NINE WORLDS TO WIN

NINE WORLDS TO WIN

Floyd McClung Jr – Kalafi Moala

WORD PUBLISHING

WORD (UK) Ltd
Milton Keynes, England

WORD AUSTRALIA
Heathmont, Victoria, Australia

STRUIK CHRISTIAN BOOKS (PTY) LTD
Maitland, South Africa

ALBY COMMERCIAL ENTERPRISES PTE LTD
Balmoral Road, Singapore

CHRISTIAN MARKETING NEW ZEALAND LTD
Havelock North, New Zealand

JENSCO LTD
Hong Kong

SALVATION BOOK CENTRE
Malaysia

NINE WORLDS TO WIN

First published by YWAM.

This edition by WORD (UK) Ltd.

ISBN 0–85009–307–4

Cover design: Bart Repko
Photographs: Dennis Fahringer

Typesetting by Suripace Ltd, Milton Keynes.
Reproduced, printed and bound in Great Britain for Word (UK) Ltd., by Cox & Wyman Ltd., Reading.

To our friends and co-workers
who have dedicated their lives to
making Jesus Christ known.

GRATEFUL ACKNOWLEDGEMENTS

We wish to thank Bart Repko for the cover design, Theo Aerts for his commitment to see this book published, Geoff Benge for helping us to get our message on paper, and Christine Alexander and Teresa Wenzl for their service in typing and editing this manuscript. Thank you!

FOREWORD

Through reading the book *Living On The Devil's Doorstep* (The McClung Family Story) I have come to know and appreciate the life and ministry of Floyd McClung. Although I have never met his family, his wife Sally, and his children Misha and Matthew, yet is seems that I have known them all along.

What struck me deeply is the boundless and irrepressible love and devotion Floyd has toward the young people of today. Both he and his family took up the cross and followed the steps and needs of a seeking but often disillusioned generation, from America to India, Nepal, Afghanistan and Amsterdam. Even when I was reading I found myself saying, "if only every young person in the world could read this book."

In fact, I am using the book for our family reading material and ask my freshman son Jerome to tell the story, three chapters at a time. He did it with interest and candor. And I can see this true life story is making an impact on him.

And now I am privileged to preview the manuscripts of *Nine Worlds to Win* by Floyd and Kalafi Moala. It is a thrilling proposition for world missions. The total task of world evangelization is being divided into nine "worlds" – Islam, Communist, Hindu, Buddhist, Tribal, Poor and Needy, Children, Urban and Nominal Christians.

This is a simple and practical approach to an immensely complex spiritual warfare. But it could and must be done. Christ commissioned it. We as soldiers of the cross have no choice but to obey His command. And this booklet could serve as an effective and useful reference to church and para-church leaders as well as individual Christians who are committed to the fulfilment of the Great Commission.

May God bless you as you read this book and as you share it with others.

Thomas Wang
International Director
Lausanne Committee for World Evangelization

TABLE OF CONTENTS

Foreword by Thomas Wang   9

Part One: An Inheritance To Claim

1 Commitment To Completion   15
2 Possessing Our Inheritance   19
3 Ready, Fire, Aim!   27
4 Non-Westerners And The Great Commission   43

Part Two: The Nine Worlds

5   The Poor And Needy   53
6   The Urban World   59
7   Children – The Small Half Of The World   67
8   The World Of Islam   73
9   The Buddhist World   79
10 The Hindu World   83
11 The World Of Tribal Peoples   87
12 Nominal Christians Of The World   91
13 The Communist World   95

Part Three: Practical Steps For Getting Involved

14 Getting The Most From Short-Term Missions   103
15 Keeping The Fire Burning   109
16 Mission Agencies – Making The Right Choice   121

Appendices

Appendix 1: The Local Church, The Mission Church
    and the Great Commission: A Tension Examined   133
Appendix 2: Short-Term Missions and the Local Church   141
Appendix 3: Mission Agencies Address List   151

Part One

An Inheritance To Claim

Chapter One

Commitment To Completion

Floyd McClung and Kalafi Moala

There was a time when missionaries weren't fashionable. They were seen as eccentrics in thread-bare suits who escaped from a world they could not come to terms with to the dark recesses of the Amazon jungle. Today, things have changed. There are still distorted views of missionaries, but ever-increasing numbers of sharp, dedicated people are becoming aware of and involved in world missions. In our mission, Youth With A Mission, we have seen rapid growth since 1980, and we receive a constant flow of requests from thousands of people each year for information about our training schools and how they can become involved in world missions.

This interest is not just in Youth With A Mission. Many denominations and mission agencies are experiencing rapid growth. At the present growth rate there will be 100,000 missionaries sent out from Third World countries alone by the year 2000. The number of North American Protestant missionaries has increased by 80% in the last decade, growing from 37,056 to 67,242.

This surge of missions activity has resulted in unprecedented growth in the church. Of the world's 5.2 billion people, one-third call themselves Christians, and half of these are believers in faith and practice. About 14,000 people are converted to Christ daily. There are 1,500,000 worship centers and congregations scattered around the globe and 1,600 new local churches are started every day. One group in Brazil is starting 8 new churches every hour!

There are 1,450 Christian radio and television outlets touching 990,000 listeners every month. 111,000,000 Bibles, or portions of scripture, are distributed annually in thousands of languages. Seventy-two percent of the world's population, according to missions research expert David Barrett, has heard the gospel, though certainly not all have responded.

This book is born out of this renewed zeal for world missions. It is a call to action. It is a presentation of the challenge before every Christian in relation to missions and evangelism. In this book we examine nine separate "worlds" that, when put together, make up our world as we know it. There is the World of Islam, the Communist World, Hindu World, Buddhist World, the World of Tribal Peoples, Poor and Needy, Children – the small half of the world, the Urban World, and the nominal Christians of the World. As we look at each of these worlds we will isolate particular challenges that we, as the church, must respond to if we are to see them evangelized.

Much has been done in missions and evangelism over the last 2000 years, but, as we shall see, much remains to be done. Yet, at no other point in church history have we had the resources and wherewithal to see the job completed. Advances in technology, missions strategies, and numbers of people involved have put completion of the great commission within reach. Only one thing is keeping us from completing the great commission: total dedication to the task.

What do we mean by completing the great commission? We are not utopians or idealists. We do not think completing the great commission will turn the world into a heaven on earth. Nor are we speaking of predicting the end of the world, or forcing the return of the Lord Jesus Christ. What we mean by completing the great commission is that every person on earth will have had the opportunity to hear, understand, and respond to the gospel, and that everyone, regardless of geographic or cultural location, will have access to a viable, evangelizing local church. There is much that is being done in missions around the world, but it is not enough just to preach the gospel. We must leave some living witness to the power of Jesus Christ in every community where we preach, and that living witness is a thriving, evangelizing church – a church that can carry on with the task of winning the lost and discipling them.

A world map masks the tremendous cultural and ethnic diversity of our world. Instead of being made up of about 175 more-or-less autonomous nations, our world is made up of between twelve to twenty-four thousand separate people groups. Experts still argue over the exact number depending upon the particular criteria they have used to arrive at their figure. Of these people groups, some 17,000, accounting for approximately two billion people, are considered to be unreached.

The Lausanne Committee on World Evangelization defines a people group as, "A significantly large grouping of individuals who perceive themselves to have a common affinity for one another, because of their shared language, religion, ethnicity, residence, occupation, class or caste, situation, or combination of these". They go on to further classify an unreached people group as, "A people group within which there is no indigenous community of believing Christians able to evangelize this group."

So, in talking of unreached people groups we are talking of a group of people who need to be the objects of not only evangelism, but also of church planting. They need among them Christian structures that can establish and disciple them in the faith, and will serve as catalysts for further evangelism among that group.

The Bengalis of Calcutta, the Malays of Malaysia and the

Himarima of the Amazon Basin in Brazil are all examples of unreached people groups that need to be reached with the gospel and have churches established among them.

This people group concept is found in the Bible. Two hundred and fifty-three times the plural word "nations" is used in scripture. But the original Greek and Hebrew words that are translated "nations" in our Bible can just as easily be translated "ethnos" or ethnic groups. The idea scripture is trying to convey is that there are nations within nations, that a nation is made up of a number of separate groupings of people.

All unreached people groups fit into one or other of the "worlds" we will describe in this book. World evangelization means we must reach these worlds with the gospel. To evangelize these "worlds" we must concentrate on evangelizing the people groups that comprise them.

A particular unreached people group may be located half way round the world or in your own city or nation. The location is not important. What is important is that we do something toward seeing these 17,000 unreached people groups reached with the gospel. Already a great number of these groups have been engaged or targeted for evangelism and church planting by various mission agencies and churches, but more needs to be done.

There are no long lists of strategies in this book, our intention is to highlight areas of need. We pray God will challenge your heart as you read it. If He speaks to you about involvement in world missions and evangelism you will find Part Three of this book helpful in following through on that call and entering into the destiny God has for your life.

Chapter Two

Possessing Our Inheritance

Kalafi Moala

"The men of Ephraim, though armed with bows, turned back on the day of battle; they did not keep God's covenant and refused to live by His law. They forgot what He had done, the wonders He had shown them" (Psalm 78:9 NIV).

The men of Ephraim were mighty warriors. They loved to fight, and were not afraid of a battle. Indeed, Moses says of the men of Ephraim, "In majesty he is like a firstborn bull; his horns are the horns of a wild ox, with them he will gore the nations, even those at the ends of the earth. Such are the ten thousands of Ephraim" (Deuteronomy 33:17). Yet, on the day of battle they turned back. They turned back not because of lack of ability or prowess in battle, but because they had failed to keep God's covenant and live by His laws. They lost sight of all God had done for them in the past, and so, on the day of battle, lost heart. They became satisfied and preoccupied with their accomplishments. They were taken up with the possessions, land, and money that previous battles had brought them, and in their preoccupation tragically forgot God.

The church in the western world is much like the men of Ephraim. We have become preoccupied with ourselves, our past achievements, and our possessions. We are consumed with building bigger and better churches, developing more and more programs, and raising huge amounts of money to keep it all going. We have lost our focus. Church buildings and programs that were once means have now become ends. Raising finances to pay for these things has replaced evangelism and discipleship as the main concern of many church leaders. Huge amounts of resources and energy are being expended to fight the wrong battle. God is first interested in people, more than elaborate buildings, full programs, and balanced budgets.

At the Day of Judgement, the people we have won to the Lord and discipled, and not the church buildings we have built, or the programs we have run, will stand as testimonies to how we lived our Christian lives. Yes, we need buildings and programs and money, but we must never lose sight of the fact that they are only means in the cause of evangelism and discipleship.

Psalm 2:8 tells us that the nations are God's inheritance for the church, the ends of the earth her possession.

There is a difference between "possession" and "inheritance". Possession has to do with what we have "now", and inheritance with what we have been promised in the "future". Our inheritance is something we do not yet have.

How tragic it would be to become so preoccupied with our possessions – what we have thus far accomplished – that we miss the inheritance God has for us. We, as His church, have an inheritance to possess, and we must reach out and possess it for God.

Our God-given inheritance is the nations, the peoples of the earth who have not yet been penetrated with the redeeming gospel of Jesus Christ. Penetrating these peoples with the gospel is the task we must become immediately preoccupied with if we are to be the finishers of the great commission in our generation. It is so easy to become preoccupied with the present that we miss the future.

There are three things we must do if we are to possess our inheritance. First, we must renew our covenant with the

Lord. After Joshua had led the Children of Israel into the promised land he did not hold a big celebration party and tell the people to relax and take it easy. Rather, he took out his knife and sharpened it and said, "Welcome to the promised land – circumcision time!" Joshua led the Children of Israel as they renewed their covenant to the Lord and prepared themselves for what lay ahead. They had arrived in the promised land, the land which was their inheritance, but they had not yet possessed it. There were others who lived there, whom they first had to subdue and conquer before they could possess their inheritance.

Renewing our covenant with God means a fresh commitment to Him, to His will, His purpose, and His unchanging character. It means a commitment to fulfilling His word. And it means to us in this generation a fresh commitment to completing the task closest to His heart – world evangelization.

We need to make to God the commitment of heart that puts our life itself on the altar of His disposal. Then, wherever, whenever, and whatever He asks us to do, we jump to attention, and, in obedience, follow His commands. When we are prepared to make this kind of sacrificial commitment to God we will be able to easily reach those peoples who are still un-evangelized.

The second thing we must do to possess our inheritance is to concentrate on what remains to be done. That is, we need to focus our attention on the "unfinished" task, instead of the "finished" task.

The words of the great missionary statesman Oswald J. Smith still ring true, "Why should anyone hear the Gospel time after time when there are those who have never heard it once?" While the second coming of Christ is today debated in many theological circles, over half of the world's population still has not heard about His first coming. Preoccupation with our possessions has hindered us from going forth and claiming our inheritance.

We must find out what needs to be done to complete the

task, and then busy ourselves completing it. Completing the task consists of reaching every unreached people group, tribe, culture and language group with the gospel. It means going to every person on earth who has not yet heard the gospel and presenting it to them.

We must go about completing the task with the tenacity of the Apostle Paul. His driving passion was frontier missions. He was always pushing on to the next frontier. To the Corinthians he wrote, "so that we can preach the gospel in the regions beyond you. For we do not want to boast about work already done in another man's territory" (2 Cor. 10:16 NIV). To the Romans he says, "It has always been my ambition to preach the gospel where Christ was not known . . ." (Rom. 15:20 NIV). This is the tenacity and drive we must have if we are to possess our inheritance.

The third thing we must do to possess our inheritance is involve ourselves in what God is doing in the nations. The Children of Israel had to involve themselves in the task of conquering and driving out those who already lived in the land they were to inherit. They could not possess the land until they had done so. Likewise, we must be actively involved in the battle to possess our inheritance.

We possess the nations and claim our inheritance by evangelizing them. What is needed today is for a great outpouring of active and aggressive evangelism around the world. World evangelization is the job of all Christians, and not just a few trained professional evangelists. If we want to possess our inheritance, then we must commit ourselves to seeing the world evangelized. This may mean that we are to go and evangelize in another nation, or that we are to begin reaching out to the ethnic groups which live in our local community, or that we commit daily to pray for and support those who are actively involved in evangelism. Perhaps we are to give sacrificially to help support a missionary. What exactly it is we commit to do is between us and the Lord. What is imperative is that we do something of significant value toward possessing our inheritance and seeing the world won for Christ.

The decade of the 1990's is going to be the missions and evangelism decade of this century. Already God is stirring the nations and producing a hunger for the gospel. As a fore-shadowing of what God will do during the 1990's, we have seen what He has done in China – doors that were previously closed have begun to open. God is going to do similar things in other Communist lands and in the Muslim world and the Hindu world. We are going to see around the world unprecedented hunger for the gospel. If we want to be a part of what God is going to do, then we must stir ourselves to action. We cannot afford to concentrate on the obstacles: closed, repressive governments, cultural and language differences, inexperience and the like. Instead, we must have our eyes fixed firmly upon the Lord and allow Him to go before us. If we fail to keep our eyes on Jesus, then like the Ephraimites, we will lose heart and flee in the face of the battle.

The church often talks about missions and expends great energy to keep the missions budget on track, but little activity seems to result. What seems to develop in the minds of many Christians is what I call the "missiological mindset". Somehow, as we talk and think about missions, we begin to believe we are actively involved in helping to fulfil the great commission, when in fact we are doing nothing other than thinking and talking about it. These are passive endeavours. God wants people who are willing to put their feet where their mouth is and go and become actively involved in evangelism and missions, and see the great commission completed. There is no room for armchair quarterbacks in the church or in missions. God wants people who will rise up, regardless of the sacrifices, and get involved with Him in seeing that every man and woman on this earth has the opportunity to hear the gospel at least once in his or her life. We must beware of becoming "missiolocially minded". What is needed is a mindset that translates into effective action on the mission field, be that mission field our own home town or on the other side of the world. Our inheritance is possessed through direct and deliberate action.

In relation to evangelism and missions, I believe the church should be like an arrow. At the tip or point of the arrow are the evangelists and the pioneer apostles. The shaft of the arrow consists of prophets, teachers, pastors, and others involved in support ministries. The evangelists and pioneer apostles penetrate new areas with the gospel, while those who make up the shaft of the arrow help in establishing the evangelistic work that has been done. This pattern is found in the Book of Acts. On the day of Pentecost, Peter stood and preached and saw 3000 people accept Jesus and be baptized, but the other apostles consolidated and built what happened that day into a church. Likewise, Philip in Samaria in Acts 8 saw multitudes respond to the message he preached, but Peter and John came and consolidated and established a church upon the foundation of converts Philip had made. Indeed, the Lord called Philip out from the revival to go and preach the gospel to an Ethiopian.

The pattern of the New Testament Church is still a good pattern to follow today. We need to be releasing teams consisting of evangelists and those with apostolic ministries who can build and establish a church out of the fruit of the evangelism.

The evangelist's commitment to a particular people or place may be short-term, and often is a moment of evangelism as on the day of Pentecost, or with Philip in Samaria, that sets the stage for the establishing of a church. The commitment of those with the pioneering gift who come to establish the church and build on the groundwork done by the evangelist is for a much longer term. Establishing a church takes time.

The evangelist and the pioneer need each other. Without the apostolic ministry, the evangelist would have few lasting results to show for his effort, and without the evangelist to penetrate and open people to the gospel, the work of the apostle in establishing a church would be all the more difficult. They need each other and they must keep each other in balance. An arrow that is all tip will not fly and an arrow that does not have a point to penetrate is useless.

We must see a mighty release of this type of ministry from the church if we are to see the great commission completed and our inheritance possessed. It may be that some churches have the necessary resources and man-power to do this of their own accord. Others may not and will want to work through the channels of existing missions, organizations and other ministries. How it is facilitated is not important, what is important is that we do it.

As the church and as individual Christians, we have an inheritance. To possess our inheritance we need to renew our covenant with God, concentrate on the unfinished task, and get involved in winning the lost. This world is ready for, and needs, a great outpouring of aggressive evangelism.

Chapter Three

Ready, Fire, Aim!

Floyd McClung

Imagine a man about to go target shooting. He takes his rifle from its cabinet, loads it with a bullet, and heads out to the back of the barn. He lifts the rifle carefully to his shoulder, aims and fires. Triumphantly he marches to the barn and paints a huge target. Working carefully he makes sure the bulls-eye is precisely over the bullet hole in the side of the barn. Then, with an exultant shout he announces loudly to passersby, "Look, I hit the bull's-eye."

"Ridiculous," you say, "you put the target up first and then shoot at it. Without a target it's pointless, you're aiming at nothing." This is true, but sadly when it comes to evangelism and missions many of us in the church are like this "expert marksman". We aim at nothing and claim to hit everything. We expend much money, time and energy in frantic activity without any certainty as to whom we are trying to reach and the best way to do so.

We are not targeted, and there is a great need in the Body of Christ today to be focused in our efforts to reach people. As we will see in this book, there are worlds to be won before the great commission can be completed. By clearly targeting one of these unreached worlds, and a particular people group or city within it, we will begin to see significant advances toward completing the great commission.

What does it mean to be targeted or focused? Being focused involves four things: knowing whom we are trying to reach with the gospel, having a time frame within which to do it.

We must know who our audience is. Perhaps they are a particular people group, a city, or a group of people of common identity within the city. We must remember that in choosing who our audience should be, the more distinct the group is, the greater the chances of being successful and achieving what it is we want to achieve. So to choose a whole nation may not really be targeting, while choosing within that nation a smaller group, say, immigrants from Morocco, would be aiming at a target.

We need clear objectives. What is it we want to occur in our audience? Do we want to commit their lives to the Lord, or see a church established among them? Do we want to see these people discipled? The results we want to occur are our objectives. It is not enough just to speak the good news. We must work for results.

Having established our audience and objectives, we will then want to establish the strategies we are going to employ to achieve our objectives. The strategies may be ones other people have used successfully in the past, or they may be completely new. God will give us new ways to reach people as we think, listen, research and pray. Whatever the strategy is, we must keep in mind the geographic and cultural location of the people we want to reach. A strategy that is effective for reaching teenagers in the United States with the gospel may not have the same results in Ethiopia. Our strategy must be a personal and relevant response to the people we are called to share the gospel with. What are the felt needs of the group we want to reach? How can we best attend to those needs? What strategy will both meet their needs and at the same time present them with the gospel? Finding the right approach to employ is an important key in ministering to the people effectively.

Lastly, we must consider the time frame in which we will be working and the results we expect to occur in that time. How long do we estimate this project will take? Do we expect to see dramatic results in a short amount of time? Having specific, measurable goals in mind help us chart our progress and test our effectiveness. If we expected to see dramatic results after two years, and now five years later we have yet to see any measurable results, we can safely say we have not achieved our objective and need to re-evaluate our strategies. Something must change or we must know clearly from the Lord that we are to continue. If there are no visible results from our ministry it may be because it is a tough situation and requires lots of prayer and patience. It may also be because we have been insensitive to the culture or unwise in our communications.

When I first moved to Amsterdam in the early nineteen seventies, my desire was to reach the city for Christ. Indeed, that still is my desire. However, Amsterdam is a large, culturally and ethnically diverse city. We began to target particular groups within the city and began reaching out to them. At first we reached out to the people who worked in or frequented the red light district. As time went by and God sent us more workers, we were able to target other groups and begin reaching out to them. Through this process we are today targeting and reaching out to eleven different ethnic and sub-cultural people groups, including Moroccans, Turks, Ethiopians, Chinese, Spaniards, children, tourists, street people, Dutch working people, and youth. Many have come to know Christ and new fellowships and Bible studies have been started for each of these groups. Indeed, we are seeing encouraging results as a result of our labor.

Why target?

No one group or church can reach the whole world. World evangelism is rather like building a hundred-foot-wide brick wall across Canada. No one person can do it alone. It requires joint effort. It requires a large number of people each doing their part to build the wall a brick at a time. The task will be completed by churches and Christian organizations each doing, to the best of their abilities, what they are able. The particular people group we choose to reach with the gospel is like another brick added towards completing the task.

Targeting is the wisest use of the resources God has given to us. By trying to reach the whole world alone we spread our resources so thinly that we end up achieving very little. We cannot paint a skyscraper with a gallon of paint. No matter how much we thin it down it will not do the job. No one local church or mission agency has the resources to reach the whole world and complete the great commission. No matter how thin their resources are spread, they will not get the job done. But, just as a gallon of paint will cover a small room, so the resources that each church possess are adequate to reaching a particular people group.

If we all target different people groups and do our part toward reaching them with the gospel, we could see the great commission completed within a reasonably short period of time. I have faith to believe that God wants this to happen. He has certainly made it clear in His word that this is what He wants! (Matthew 24:14; 28:18-19). If every Christian group and church were to cooperate and each target an area or people group that no one else has targeted to evangelise, the task would soon be completed. What slows completion of the great commission is massive duplication of effort, and failure to target.

Without aiming our evangelistic programs in local churches and educational institutions at a target, they can easily become ends in themselves. Without specifically committing ourselves to people outside our circle of activity, we turn inward and our programs become the most important thing to us. This is particularly true in the area of education and training. Often out of necessity to be more effective in reaching a particular people group we develop a training program. With a specific goal in mind the program is effective. However, there is a tendency, over time, for programs to become entrenched. We continue running our program, regardless of its effectiveness. We have done things in the past this way, so we carry right on in the present doing them the same way. When this occurs we have lost sight of our original objective and the program has become an end in itself. Education is important, but it should only be done when we have obedience as our goal. Programs which are run without definite goals and purposes in mind are only monuments to the way we do things.

Why do we fail to target?

We fail to target basically for three reasons. First, because of a fear of failure. Targeting is like putting up a sign for all to read that says, "This is what we are doing to help complete the great commission." By narrowing down our options in this way failure is a possibility. However, refusal to narrow down our options and to target will lead to certain failure. Indeed, through targeting our success is much more certain.

Fear of the unfamiliar heightens our fear of targeting. In reaching out to people across cultural boundaries we enter into the unfamiliar. We are more comfortable and at ease in our own culture. We understand the way things are done, the way decisions are made, and why people think the way they do. In entering another culture we leave that knowledge behind. There is no easy way around this fear other than trusting the Lord. If He has called us to reach a particular people group with the gospel, then we must trust Him to open doors through which we can do it. We can, of course, minimize our sense of the unfamiliar by learning the language of the people we want to reach and by taking the time to understand and enter into their culture. It is much more comfortable to stay at home, but real success and blessing goes to those who are willing to venture into the unknown at the Lord's beckoning.

Second, we don't target because we don't think targeting is the spiritual thing to do. But nothing could be further from the truth. Nehemiah is an example of a man who knew how to target. He had a job to do: re-build the city wall of Jerusalem. The first thing he did was pray. He asked God to move on his behalf so that he could get to Jerusalem. After arriving in Jerusalem, he set about inspecting the wall and sizing up what needed to be done to re-build it. Having done this he gave each man a work assignment. Each man was not required to build the whole wall, only a small bit of it. Thus, as each man completed his assignment, bit by bit the wall was re-built and the job completed. Through prayer, research, and common sense Nehemiah was able to complete the task of re-building the city wall of Jerusalem. Nehemiah was single-minded. He set goals and he worked toward them; and he was rewarded with success.

The third reason why we don't target is because of a lack of courage and determination. In Judges 18, the Danites are looking for land to claim as their inheritance. Instead of asking God what portion of the land He wanted them to inherit, they sent out spies to find the easiest piece of land to conquer and claim as their inheritance. They ended up fighting the wrong battle and taking land that wasn't their inheritance. As a result, they fell into idolatry.

We in the church have a tendency to be like the Danites. Redeeming the nations of the world is the battle God has for us. Yet, all to often, we take the easy ground -- a bigger and better church, a full schedule of programs, and a more comfortable lifestyle. We fool ourselves into thinking these things are our inheritance, but there is much more to life than these things. People are our inheritance. It is people, not programs or church architecture that God will judge on the Day of Judgement. How sad it would be to stand before Christ on that day and see people going to eternity lost, because we had been so busy fighting the wrong fight.

Completing the Commission

With faith and God's blessing, we must ask ourselves if it is possible in principle to ever complete the great commission. With the resources and technology that is available to us, with so many people committed to serve, what is keeping us from fulfilling the great commission? Completion of the Lord's last commandment is not just dependent on God's sovereignty. What is needed is total dedication to the task.

It certainly is not due to a lack of zeal. At present there are 406 plans to evangelize the whole world. In total, there have been over 700 of these plans, according to David Barrett, going back to the 18th Century. Here is a list of major plans for world evangelization that are current and active:

Origin	Name of Ongoing committee/program
1961	Commission on World Mission and Evangelism
1964	Secretariat for Non-Christians
1965	Synod of Bishops (Synodus Episcoporum)
1967	Congregation of the Evangelization of Peoples
1971	World Evangelization Strategy Consultation
1976	Strategy Working Group
1978	Great Commission Strategy Resource Network
1981	World Evangelism Strategy Work Group
1981	World Evangelism Committee
1982	Project 223
1984	Strategy to Every People (STEP) Programme
1985	Orthodox Task Force/Advisory Group
1985	Global Evangelization Strategy Consultation
1985	Global Strategy Commission
1986	Global Strategy Group

1986	Total Church Evangelization Strategy Committee
1986	World Evangelization Strategy Committee
1986	Evangelization 2000
1987	Charismatics United for World Evangelization
1987	Interdenominational Global Missions Conferences
1988	Global Consultation on AD 2000 and Beyond
1988	New Life 2000

Other Plans:
The World By 2000

Most of these plans focus on the year 2000 as a date to work towards for completion. For example: "The World by 2000" is sponsored by four international broadcasting agencies (TWR, REBC, HCJB and ELWA). A statement jointly signed by the leaders of these agencies say, "We are committed to provide every man, woman, and child on earth the opportunity to turn on their radio and hear the gospel of Jesus Christ in a language they can understand, so they can become followers of Christ and responsible members of His church. We plan to complete this task by the year 2000."

Bold Mission Thrust

Bold Mission Thrust is the Southern Baptist strategy for world evangelization which gives emphasis to discipling and evangelizing.

Indeed, it has been labelled as "one of history's most extensive, most organized, most detailed, and most determined evangelistic plans." Its oft-repeated objective is to enable every person in the world to hear and respond to the gospel of Christ by the year 2000.

DAWN Movement

DAWN (Discipling A Whole Nation) is committed to finding visionaries in every country of the world by 1995 that they can train to help lead the way in discipling a whole nation.

Evangelization 2000

Roman Catholics are planning a one billion dollar project called Evangelization 2000, as reported by Julia Duin in the News Section of Christianity Today (February 6, 1987). The ten-year project will culminate in a world-wide satellite telecast on Christmas Day in the year 2000 when Pope John Paul II, or his successor, will speak to a potential audience of at least 5 billion people.

Mission 2000

The U.S. Centre for World Mission (USCWM) is working on a 15-year plan called Mission 2000 to chart the course of a cooperative mission effort to evangelize the world.

Into Every Home By 2000

This is a plan by World Literature Crusade (now called Every Home for Christ) aimed at placing a piece of Christian literature in every home on earth by AD 2000. They have reached 680 million homes in the last 30 years. They are at present reaching 500,000 more homes each month. There are a total of 1 billion, 700 million homes and this number is growing by 30 million each year due to the population explosion.

Global Evangelism Movement

A new term has been coined by David Barrett to describe the phenomenon of all the plans to evangelize the world:

The Global Evangelism Movement (GEM). But Barrett also cautions us: throughout the history of the church there have been at least 700 plans for world evangelization. Most of them have fizzled out and about 30 of them are still active today. What were the reasons for failures? "Perhaps the major reason for the failure has been the absence of any attempt either to structure the objective or to deal realistically with the major obstacles . . .Pious hopes have been allowed to substitute for determined organizational and logistical investigation and action on the part of thoroughly well-informed global missions leaders meeting and acting regularly together, with all the facts in front of them. We need to structure this global movement somewhat more realistically," says Barrett. He goes on to say, "What can be done about this unsatisfactory situation? The value of our analysis is that it provides us with ways forward. Having completed our own range of forecasts, we now realize that the major obstacle is the ignorance all such plans have of each other, and their failure to work together, to mesh in any degree, or to be globally co-ordinated. A completely new and unprecedented type of initiative is needed which, while recognizing the autonomy of all existing plans, overcomes this reluctance by bringing them into close touch with each other in the total global North/South and East/West context."

Matthew 28:19-20 makes it clear that it is the Lord's intention that the church in every generation should reach its generation with the gospel. We should not feel we are bringing world history to an end by focusing on completion.

We will simply be doing what every generation should have done, and keep on doing it until the Lord returns. There is no place for pride in doing what we should do in obedience to our Lord.

When we refer to completion by the year 2000, we are not speaking of a prediction, but a projection. If we don't set a specific goal, we will have nothing specific to pray for, work for and judge ourselves by to see if we are on course.

If world evangelization is to become a reality, we must earnestly pray for a deep move of God's Spirit to shake and stir His church world-wide. Luis Bush of Partner's International says, "History demonstrates and scripture (Acts 1:8) affirms that any major initiative in world missions must be preceded by a spiritual revival and renewal in the Church. The Church must grasp the fullness of the power of the Spirit of God before expecting to launch out in a fresh outreach. There is a definite cause-effect relationship between the increased activity of the Spirit of God in the Church and the outreach to the world."

This must also be accompanied by each part of the church on each continent owning the vision and contributing its part. Increased consultation between leaders, respect, encouragement, and co-operation must take place in a non-structured, Spirit-led fashion. This must be done in close contact with the researchers collecting and feeding back data so we can keep abreast of where God's Spirit is moving and where the spiritual attacks are also coming.

If we do this in a spirit of love and co-operation, with much humility and forbearance for one another, God will enable His church to reach every creature with the gospel. It is God's will!

After extensive research, David Barrett has tried to help the church see the world more clearly in terms of what still needs to be done to complete the great commission.

Ed Dayton of World Vision summarizes Barrett's research in his letter *The Cutting Edge*. He refers to the diagram found overleaf:

"At the bottom of the globe is THE CHRISTIAN WORLD.

"In the center is the EVANGELIZED NON-CHRISTIAN WORLD. The top section shows the UNEVANGELIZED (or unreached) WORLD.

"This unevangelized world is then depicted as embracing three kinds of segments: 2,000 PEOPLES (a human population with a common language, shared ethnicity, and significant patterns of social interaction), 1,000 METROPOLISES, and 30 COUNTRIES. These segments obviously overlap. Within an unevangelized country there may be both unevangelized peoples and major cities. But this overlap need not concern us if we use the concept to ensure that some body of Christians has in its mind a desire to see one of these major segments evangelized."

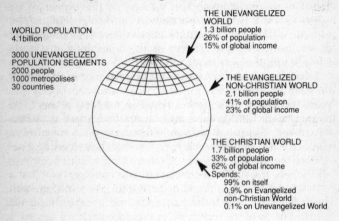

WORLD POPULATION
4.1 billion

3000 UNEVANGELIZED
POPULATION SEGMENTS
2000 people
1000 metropolises
30 countries

THE UNEVANGELIZED
WORLD
1.3 billion people
26% of population
15% of global income

THE EVANGELIZED
NON-CHRISTIAN WORLD
2.1 billion people
41% of population
23% of global income

THE CHRISTIAN WORLD
1.7 billion people
33% of population
62% of global income
Spends:
  99% on itself
  0.9% on Evangelized
  non-Christian World
  0.1% on Unevangelized World

Who Is Trying To Reach Them?

"What this concept does is give us a basis for sharing information as to who is targeting a major group, city, or country that is without any gospel witness. It permits us to match agencies with a segment and thus to know who is attempting to work among each segment. It gives us a reasonable basis for co-operation in sharing information that we may have about any one of the segments, information that will help others to do a better job.

"Matching agencies with a particular segment does not imply comity or exclusiveness. We are not saying that because one agency is concerned for one of these major segments, that others should not be. Quite the opposite!

There are many different agencies with different ministries.

"Church planting, scripture distribution and translation, radio broadcasting, tentmaking and many other ministries all have their place.

"Knowing what has been done and what is being done gives us the basis for doing a better job and allocating our resources more effectively.

"And it helps us to communicate progress against the ultimate goal of world evangelization. Instead of publishing an Unreached Peoples Directory of those with no efforts being made to reach them, we can now list agencies who have begun or, at the very least, indicate there are one or more efforts underway."

It is possible! With God's help, we can reach the 2,000 people groups, 1,000 cities and 30 countries that are basically unevangelized. As Ed Dayton suggests, it is time for us to share what we are doing with one another so we can cooperate more closely.

To speak of completing the great commission is not just a commitment to a superficial presentation of a cheap gospel. The Lord Jesus is not just interested in the breadth of our vision, but also the depth of our involvement in people's lives.

His example is our model. He gave up everything, left His "home" and all that went with it, and lived simply and compassionately with His own family and with those He came to serve.

The incarnational approach is essential to world evangelism. We must enter cultures and care for people in sensitivity, not in arrogance. We must live amongst people, adapting to their culture and lifestyle. The people we are called to are not to be seen as the objects of our evangelistic programs, but as our friends. We must come to learn before we attempt to teach. We must affirm what is good, not just look for what is bad. Jesus did not die for the cause of world evangelization, but for people. Yet, we also know that He died for all people, the whole world.

Dangers and Blessings

There are both dangers and blessings in seeking to fulfil the great commission by AD 2000. If we are motivated by pride, a date, or any other concern other than a compassion for the lost, we will do more harm than good.

God does not need more "do-gooders" in the world but He does want more people from all nations going to all nations, who love Him and who proclaim the good news in word and deed.

If setting a faith goal produces programs that are insensitive to people, that are more concerned with reaching a certain number of people than caring personally for individuals, then the global evangelization movement is a danger, not a blessing. We cannot predict the return of our Lord. The times and seasons are in His hands. We cannot complete the great commission in our own strength, no matter how much money and no matter how many people get involved.

We are desperately dependent on the Lord for everything we do.

But if it is His will, and He enables us and multiplies our efforts, we can reach every person with the gospel.

We must choose carefully our motives, and must be prepared to adjust our goals along the way. If it becomes apparent in 1995 that we won't make our goal, lets adjust and lengthen the time frame back to AD 2010. But let us not hold back from trying, out of concern for making mistakes or being disappointed.

Is it not the Lord who is stirring our hearts to trust Him for every person to have the opportunity to know of His love?

Total Commitment to Completion

This single-mindedness and dedication to the task is perhaps nowhere better portrayed than in the lives of two officers, George Pollard and Edward Wright, who were sent from England in 1883 to "take New Zealand for Christ", as commanded by General Booth. After a short trip in Australia, where they searched out three recruits to go with them, they set sail for Dunedin, New Zealand. On the way Pollard told Wright, "You go to Auckland in the far north, and I'll go to Dunedin in the south; we'll work toward Wellington, and shake hands when we get there."

They arrived in New Zealand in April, 1883, and as arranged, three of them began their work in Dunedin, and the other two went to Auckland. Nine months later, when the Salvation Army in New Zealand held its first Congress, there were thirty officers, mostly New Zealanders, and five hundred soldiers who had signed up to work full-time. In nine months the Salvation Army had made and established over 5,000 converts! It was the greatest revival in the history of New Zealand. The impact of the team was on the front pages of the newspapers for months. They literally "took New Zealand for Christ!"

There is a world to win, and you have a vital part to play in winning it. If we each do our part, and step out in faith to claim our specific inheritance in humility and purity, God will give us the victory.

Are you prepared, right now, to commit your life to completing the great commission in obedience to our Lord Jesus Christ, wherever that takes you, whatever you will do, wherever God calls you?

Chapter Four

Non-Westerners And The Great Commission

Kalafi Moala

The most significant phenomenon in missions as we move down the road toward completion of the great commission is the emerging missionary movements from the non-western world, and the thousands of non-western missionaries sent out from these nations. It is estimated that by the year 2000 60% of the world's Christians will be non-westerners. The biggest churches in the world are non-western. The countries that are experiencing explosive Christian growth are in the non-western world. In Asia, Latin America and Africa the harvest is riper than in any other part of the world.

Nigeria is no longer a country which just receives missionaries, it is a country which sends missionaries out all over the world. There are many North American missionaries in Brazil, but Brazil also sends missionaries to the ends of the earth. The Philippines has become a major missionary-sending country. God is moving in the non-western world, turning countries that were previously mission fields into part of the mission force.

I believe we need to continue to mobilize large numbers

of Christians from the developing world into missions. Those that were once a mission field must now become part of the mission force. I don't mean that they just become involved in missions work in their own nation, but that they become involved in taking the gospel cross-culturally to other nations and people groups.

Historically, mission movements have emerged from dynamic Christian growth. Today that growth is taking place in the developing world. Latin America, Africa and Asia are all experiencing a dynamic growth and multiplication of the Christian faith. It is only natural then, that out of this great growth should emerge a mighty missions movement.

Such a movement is beginning to develop. I believe we will see it continue to grow and become a major missions movement that will carry on into the 21st century.

There are many reasons why non-western Christians from the developing world should become involved in missions. The gospel is an international gospel, it is not a western gospel. The gospel was first delivered in a non-western setting. However, when there are only western missionaries involved in the task of sharing that gospel it is soon wrapped in western philosophical and cultural concepts that become part of the gospel. With only western involvement we soon have a theology, ecclesiology, liturgy, organizational structure, and training program that are western in form, and which take much away from the gospel that was meant to be meaningful and relevant to all cultures. We need non-westerners involved in missions to give the international representation and application the gospel needs.

The centers of Christian influence in the world are shifting from the western to the non-western world. In the past, Lausanne, London, Berlin, Pasadena, and Wheaton played major roles in Christian influence. Today Singapore, Seoul, Sao Paulo, Buenos Aires, Nairobi, Suva, and Madras have become centers of Christian and missions influence. In the same way today's list of Christian leaders includes not only such names as Graham, McGravran, Winter, Stott, and Swindoll, but also Cho, Wang, Babu, Havea, and Palau.

In Genesis 12:1-3, God promises Abraham that he will be a blessing to all the peoples of the earth. Today's spiritual descendants of Abraham (those who know Jesus as their Lord) are both westerners and non-westerners. The non-western segment of Abraham's family needs to rise up and fulfil its calling to be a blessing to all the peoples of the earth.

Non westerners who become involved in missions bring with them a less-complicated faith. They are less encumbered with theological complications that are, for the most part, irrelevant to the task of reaching the unreached with the gospel. Being less encumbered often means they are more effective in reaching across cultural boundaries with the gospel.

If the gospel is to be made relevant and meaningful to those who inhabit the Muslim, Hindu, Buddhist, tribal, and urban worlds then it must be de-westernized. Those from the non-western world are particularly effective in doing this, and it must be done if we are to see a mighty penetration of the gospel into these worlds.

The majority of the world's unreached people groups are located in the developing world. Non-western missionaries are culturally and geographically closer to these groups, culturally sensitive to their need, and able to adapt more easily to their culture.

Non-western missionaries are less expensive to support on the mission field. In most cases, an Indian missionary, or a South Pacific Island missionary can live comfortably on a quarter of what it takes to support an American missionary working on the same mission field.

For these reasons non-westerners have a vital role to play, and an important contribution to make toward the task of completing the great mission. Non-westerners are needed on the mission field, and western missionaries must make a place for them.

In missions, if the church is to stay relevant and on the cutting edge of what God is doing in the world, we must de-westernize our mission organizations. We also need to see the release of many non-western ministries and missionary organizations. Non-westerners must be released into our midst to teach us and lead us into the next wave of God's missionary activity on earth.

The question that immediately arises is, how do we de-westernize our mission organizations? And how do we mobilize non-westerners onto the mission field, and facilitate them while they are there?

The first step toward de-westernizing our mission organizations is developing cross-cultural understanding. I believe a lack of this understanding is one of the reasons why there aren't more non-western missionaries on the mission field today. We must learn to enter into long and lasting relationships with our non-western co-workers. It often occurs on the mission field that western missionaries gravitate toward other western missionaries, and non-westerners are left out of more intimate levels of friendship. This is understandable as people of similar cultures naturally gravitate toward one another. But if we want non-westerners to play key roles in our mission organizations we must adopt sensitive cross-cultural ways of relating to them. Oftentimes non-westerners have to make greater cross-cultural adjustments to relate to the mission organization than they do to the people they are trying to reach.

The way we run things must also be closely examined. Are our mission centers, programs, leadership styles, training programs and management styles meaningful and relevant to non-western people? All too often, the answer is no. Most of the things we do are done with western cultural and philosophical assumptions in mind. However, westerners and non-westerners do not share the same set of cultural and philosophic assumptions about the world.

One of the reasons, I believe, there are not more non-western leaders active in mission organizations today is because we are measuring them by the wrong yardstick. We are measuring them by a western yardstick, wanting to see the qualities we consider suitable for a good leader in western society. However, if we are to measure them by a strictly biblical yardstick, and on the qualities their cultures consider to be good attributes of a leader, we would see many more non-westerners released into leadership in missions.

We must also be aware of tokenism in this area. We must raise up these leaders because they are the best men for the job, not because we want to appease our conscience and give the appearance that our organization is integrated along western-non-western lines. Nothing is more devastating to a person than knowing he has been raised to leadership simply for appearance's sake. In developing non-western leaders we must strive to build up their self-worth and confidence by raising them up because, when judged by the standards noted above, they are the best men for the job.

In the area of training for the mission field, are our modes of learning compatible with non-western learning patterns, understanding, and values? Are we propagating western values through our training? Who is conducting most of the training, westerners or non-westerners? The area of training within our mission organizations is one of the key ways to determine whether or not our organization will be western or non-western in its orientation. If we want to de-westernize our organization in a nation, we start the process with our training programs. We strip from them any western cultural biases. We pay close attention to models of learning within the nation and culture. We modify our programs to suit the local needs, and we have non-westerners, and westerners who have adapted culturally, do the instructing.

While God may use a particular person to start a missions organization, He intends those called to that organization to have ownership of it. Non-westerners must feel they are part-owners of our organizations. Often, however our organizations are so culturally removed from them that it is hard for non-westerners to be a part, let alone feel ownership, of the organization.

I have noticed within our mission that the predominant culture has been western, and in particular American, simply because it was started in the west and was staffed predominantly by westerners. For many of our mission centers in non-western countries the western culture was their dominant culture. However, major changes have been occurring in order to attract and keep non-western workers in our mission. It is very hard for non-westerners to become a part of an organization in which, even in their own nation, they have to leave behind their own culture and adopt the western culture of the mission center. We, the mission, not they, should be adapting ourselves to their culture. If we adapt to their culture, they will find it easy to be a part of our organization and feel ownership of it. We have in our mission tremendous potential to see true partnership between western and non-western missionaries in completing the great commission.

Another way we promote ownership of our organizations by non-westerners is by releasing them to pioneer and establish new works. Thus, the new work becomes theirs. Not only does this promote ownership, but it gives them the chance to succeed and even make mistakes and learn from them, as well as develop leadership skills.

To challenge and mobilize the non-western church into missions requires an investment of time, money, and personnel. We need a concerted effort to change the non-western church from a mission field mentality to a mission force mentality. How we go about this is dependent upon us first asking non-western Christians the best way to mobilize people from their nations into missions. We must pay close attention to their answer, and plan our strategies accordingly.

Releasing non-westerners into positions of leadership will also help in raising up other non-westerners and seeing this new missions movement grow. These leaders will attract others into the mission, and they in turn will attract still others. As these people become involved, westerners should be vacating and handing over positions to them. Western missionaries regularly need to ask themselves, "What am I currently doing that a non-westerner couldn't also do?"

One of the questions we must deal with in regard to mobilizing the non-western church is the area of financial support. If we simply impose on them the western financial support system that our mission uses, we will isolate non-westerners and force them out. We must look for creative new ways of supporting non-western workers. However, we must at the same time be sure these methods affirm their dignity, and do not leave them feeling like the recipients of welfare and second-class missionaries. We want to avoid establishing a welfare system through special scholarships, grants, and payments. We don't want handouts that will help them meet their obligations under our western support system. Instead, we must strive for wholly new support structures.

There is a mighty missions force ready to arise from the non-western church. What we must do is encourage it. We must esteem and affirm non-western missionaries. We need them and cannot complete the task of world evangelization without them. At the same time God wants and expects them to become involved in working to further His kingdom among the nations, and we must deliver that challenge to the non-western church. However, our effort will be in vain if we do not first set about de-westernizing our missionary organizations. Non-westerners must feel comfortable in them, and ownership of them. Completion of the great commission is the job of the whole church, western and non-western. If we are to complete the task we must work together as co-laborers. This partnership in mission is imperative and is one of the major trends in world evangelization.

Part Two

The Nine Worlds

Chapter Five

The Poor And Needy

Floyd McClung

Jeff shared with me his feeling of utter hopelessness. "I shall never forget it," he said. "I felt totally frustrated by my inadequacy to do anything. I held that small baby in my arms. Around me were ramshackle houses built from scraps of wood, plastic, iron, and cloth. Beyond I could see the piles of rotting trash and smell the acrid odor they produced. Flies, like the heavy afternoon humidity, hung in the air. All the hopelessness and despair of this environment seemed centered at that moment on the emaciated, malnourished baby that lay dying in my arms. All the help my medical colleagues had given had not been sufficient to wrench her from the jaws of imminent death. Within hours she was dead."

"Further on, we found Ronny lying in his own excrement on a dirt floor. Like the baby, he too was emaciated and suffering from among other things, severe malnutrition. No longer knowing what to do, his mother sat resolutely waiting for Ronny to die. Death is a close companion in this harsh environment. This time however, medical aid was able to pull Ronny back from certain death."

That was several years ago in the Metro Manila garbage dump where nine thousand people live atop a growing mountain of trash. I am happy to report today that the teams working there have had a significant impact upon the community. The social, moral, economic, and spiritual well-being of the community has improved. The diseases that claimed the lives of so many people there are now under control, and the malnourished are receiving the food they need. As well as this, the teams have been able to help some people find jobs or start small businesses, and others have helped in relocating off the dump. People have accepted Christ, and community Bible studies and small churches have been established. The teams have not alleviated all the needs in this community, but they have made life more bearable for many of the people who live there.

The people who live on Manila's garbage dump are just a small part of the human need that exists worldwide. Squatter and slum communities have become a fact of life in most major cities of the developing world. Manila has an estimated two million squatters scattered across the city in 415 squatter communities, while in Bangkok there are 1042 slum neighbourhoods. Similar circumstances exist in Mexico City, Cairo, Calcutta, Bombay, Jakarta and any number of other cities in the developing world.

Extreme human need is not confined only to cities. There are 18 million poor and needy people living in refugee camps around the world, and millions of people in East Africa are precariously poised on the verge of starvation as ravaging famine stalks that area of the world.

Neither is human need confined to the developing world. In Western cities people live and die on the streets. New York City has over 75,000 people who survive by rummaging through trash cans for food. Drive through the streets of downtown Los Angeles on any night and you will see row upon row of homeless people sleeping on the sidewalks. Less visible, but equally devastating, are areas of human need such as domestic violence, child abuse, drug and alcohol addiction, and the prostitutes who ply the streets of the world, ensnared and needy.

I could go on giving examples and statistics but most of us are well aware of the vast human need that exists in our world. We need only watch television or read a newspaper to see the images of human suffering: pathetic emaciated human skeletons slowly starving, people mutilated and tormented by war and injustice, whole families living in the bus depots, subways, and condemned buildings of our cities.

Each of these is a person to whom the church must respond. Jesus was touched by human need and responded to it with acts of mercy. He left us the parable of the "Good Samaritan" as an example of how He expects Christians to respond to human suffering and misfortune. As Christians, we can do no less than follow the example He has left us in word and deed.

I believe the gospel has two facets: evangelism and practical concern. In our mission, we like to call it the "two-handed gospel". What I mean by practical concern is becoming aware of specific human needs, then, in collaboration with the poor and needy, seeking solutions to those needs – solutions they can own. I am not talking about paternalism or sympathy; I'm talking about respecting the poor. We must respect them enough to listen to their understanding of their problems and together seek solutions.

We must learn to come to people in need with listening ears and respect for their perspective, and work together toward solutions. Through this approach we empower people to take control over their own lives. Poverty is more than just having no money; it is not having the freedom to make choices about one's destiny.

It takes time and sustained effort to minister in this way, but if we persevere, we will see hearts open to the gospel. A starving man in Africa told a member of one of our teams who was sharing the gospel with him, "I can't hear you, I am too hungry." How true this is. To us as Christians, a person's spiritual needs may be the most pressing and obvious, but we can never effectively minister to those without until we have first dealt with the immediate needs the individual is feeling, be that providing food, shelter, medical care, or simple respect. Meet these needs first and the person is more likely to lend a listening ear to the gospel message we have to share. Through this approach, not only do we have the chance to tell them about Jesus, we have the opportunity to actively portray His love for them.

Even if our ministry to the poor and needy cannot be as elaborate and as far-reaching as some of the community development projects being undertaken around the world, it is important we do something toward ministering to the human need that surrounds us where we live. Perhaps for us it is operating a home for unwed mothers in our town, or a feeding program for homeless people. It also means reaching out in friendship to people of other races in our city or neighbourhood. There is something hypocritical about sending money and people to other continents but never having a friendship with people of that race in our own country.

Perhaps together with other churches in the area we could sponsor a medical clinic or food program in a squatter community. The ways we can express Christ's love through acts of mercy are many and varied. The particular method we use is not as important as it is to do something about the tremendous human need and suffering everywhere.

Sadly, I have heard people in the church say, "Jesus told us the poor and the needy would always be with us; therefore, He does not want us to be too concerned about their condition. After all, no amount of effort is going to solve the problem." The people who say this have failed to see the example of Jesus. He spent His life responding and ministering to human need. No, He did not erase poverty, but that did not deter Him from reaching out in love and ministering to people. Neither will we single-handedly solve the problems of the poor and needy. We're not trying to build a utopian world. Indeed, such thinking is what Jesus was warning us about. We will not solve all mankind's problems, regardless of how much effort we apply. However, neither can we sit back and do nothing about the plight of the poor and powerless. It was Jesus who told us that in ministering to the poor that we are in fact ministering to Him (Matthew 2:4).

Many Christians, alas, have become callous to the suffering they see around them. They watch the evening news on television and see the sights and sounds of human suffering and need. At first they are horrified; they respond with concern and prayer. But, as time goes by and they are confronted with the same scenes night after night, they lose their sense of horror, their concern dwindles, and they stop praying. The tragic needs of human beings around the world become background noise they eventually fail to notice.

We could say this is to be expected since we are only human, but Jesus was never indifferent to, nor failed to recognize, human need and suffering. When confronted with it He always moved in His heart to action. We must follow His example and not allow the dictates of our human nature to shape our response to the poor and needy. Daily we need to ask God to keep our hearts soft and tender toward human need. If we become callous and fail to minister to the needy in the name of the Lord, we become hard.

I believe one of the reasons for the advance of communism is because of a failure by the church to adequately respond to the needs of people. This was driven home to me when I lived in the developing world. There I observed first-hand the plight of the poor and needy. I saw injustice. I saw pain and hopelessness. I saw people with so much money they didn't know what to do with it, and I saw people starving to death because they had so little money they could not afford food. I saw missionaries living in secluded, walled, guarded housing developments separated from the needs of the people they were trying to reach. And I saw communism on the rise. Why? Because those communists knew the felt needs of the people and promised to do something about them. Rarely did they live up to their promises, but many of the people were so desperate that a promise was better than nothing. I spoke with a well-educated Christian college student one day. She was a leader in her school and was actively evangelizing her classmates. To my surprise, as we talked about the future of her country, she told me in all sincerity that communism was the only hope for her country. She thought they were the only ones that were really concerned about the needs of the people.

I'm not trying to make a justification for communism in developing world nations, but I do want to illustrate that our failure to respond as a church to the poor and the needy has dire consequences, not only in terms of human suffering, but also in terms of the political ideologies that take root in the ferment of human suffering – ideologies that are hostile to Christianity and the spread of the gospel, particularly because they have not seen concern on the part of evangelical Christians.

We must dispel the impression that as Christians we're only interested in saving souls and building grandiose churches. It is time for us to rise up and take the love and compassion of Jesus to the poor and needy of this world. The world does not need more fancy evangelists trumpeting their messages of gospel truth mixed with slick consumerism. What the world needs is an army of caring Christians who, through mercy and love, will demonstrate Christ to the poor and needy of this world, people who will sit and listen, who will respect the poor and needy enough to learn from them, and who will respond to them in a way that affirms their dignity and value to God.

The gospel is a two-handed gospel. We cannot reach out in mercy and love effectively without evangelism, and, we cannot evangelize effectively unless we reach out in mercy and love. If we reach out with the two hands of the gospel we will see the doors of a multitude of hearts swing open to the gospel.

Chapter Six

The Urban World

Floyd McClung

Every morning 73% of Latin America's population awakens to the sights, sounds, and smells of the city. Our world is fast becoming an urban world. By the year 2010 three out of every four people on earth will live in a city. Already 79% of all Americans live in urban areas. Cities worldwide are growing at an alarming rate. Every month Mexico City, the world's second largest city with a current population of 19 million, grows by fifty to eighty thousand people, the equivalent of almost one million people a year. By the year 2000 its population will have swollen to an estimated 30 million people. Every year 750,000 people move to Bangkok, Thailand. It took Manchester, England 139 years to reach a total population of 800,000! Today there are 313 world class cities, (cities with a population of one million or more, or that have major international influence,) and by the year 2000 there will be between 500 and 750 of them. Of these 313 cities, 14 are categorized as "supercities" having a population in excess of 10 million. Of these 14 supercities, 10 are in the developing world. By the turn of the century the number will have swollen to 24 supercities, 18 of which will be in the developing world.

Today's cities are not only large, they are also ethnically

diverse and complex. In Amsterdam, where I live, there are 44 distinct ethnic neighbourhoods and over 114 different languages are spoken. In London over 120 languages are spoken, while in Los Angeles the Southern Baptist denomination worships in 52 languages every Sunday. The Los Angeles Unified School District has identified more than eighty languages spoken in its schools. Moreover, of the 600,000 children the school district encompasses, 25% have limited or no proficiency in English, and more than half of all students in the district require remedial teaching in English. Los Angeles also has the largest Mexican, Korean, Filipino, and Vietnamese metropolitan areas outside their respective countries, and the second largest Chinese and Japanese communities. Among the nearly sixty thousand residents (1980 census) that live within a one square mile area of inner-city Chicago, fifty nations of the world are represented.

Cities are experiencing rapid population growth for a number of reasons. Firstly, lack of birth control. In the developing world there is no city that has an average age above twenty years old. Lack of birth control has lead to explosive growth in the numbers of children and young people who inhabit the city. The number of people seeking steady employment and the opportunity to escape the rural poverty is rampant in so many of the developing nations. Few people, however, find what they are looking for and end up unemployed and locked into a cycle of urban poverty. In Africa, 25% of African men living in cities are unemployed, and similar figures exist for other regions of the world. People flee famine and natural disasters. In Africa and Asia whole cities have been created by refugees. Many urban dwellers have come looking for educational opportunities. Lastly, people are lured by big city life. A crowd gathers a bigger crowd, and big cities gather people who are intrigued by and drawn to the bustle of life in the city.

The city is rapidly replacing the grass huts and rural

villages of Africa and Asia as the world's single greatest mission field. Sadly, the church seems to be losing the fight for the city. Most Christians are alienated from the city and see them as godless centers of sin, death, and destruction. But that is not how God views the city.

The story of Abraham's prayer for Sodom is the first instance of God hearing and responding to an intercessor's prayer (Genesis 18 and 19). So important to God was the city that He would have spared it if there had been only ten righteous men in it.

Nineveh was the capital of Assyria. Assyrians were the most violent people of the ancient world. They were the Nazis of the Middle East – brutal, immoral, and idolatrous. Yet God cared for Nineveh so much that He sent Jonah there. He wanted the inhabitants of Nineveh to repent and turn to Him. Jonah 4:11 reveals God's heart for the city: "But Nineveh has more than a hundred and twenty thousand people that cannot tell their left hand from their right, and many cattle as well. Should I not be concerned about the great city?"

We must develop a sense of urban spirituality. We don't have to go to the forest or mountains to find God or be spiritually renewed. God is in the city. People can find Him there. This is important because if we imply to city dwellers that they have to go to the countryside to be spiritually renewed we are in essence saying to them, "In the city, God doesn't care about you." The church has for too long been sending this message to the city. Look at Christian posters and book covers. The pictures of mountains and sunsets over pristine lakes with verses on them about renewal and finding God are sending the wrong message. Our perceptions need to change. Yes, cities are centers of sin and wickedness, but so are suburbs, towns and villages. Sin is not in the environment, but in people. Cities are people, and God's heart aches for them to hear of the love He has for them. He agonizes over the human suffering and need in cities, and mourns over the callousness of His church to that suffering. Jesus wept over the spiritual condition of the city of Jerusalem. How many Christians are on their knees today, weeping over the spiritual condition of the cities of the world?

God dwells in His people, and where His people are, there He is also. God lives in the city, because His people live in the city. The city is the dwelling place of God. It is sacred because God is there. It is not the devil's, it is the Lord's. The earth is the Lord's, including the urban world.

We have also failed to see the importance of the city. Cities are more than just an amount of people living in a defined geographic area. Cities are "processes" where trends and movements are born.

What do we mean by this? Cities set the trends for the world. What takes place in the city spills over into the surrounding country and beyond. There are four major processes that occur in the city. First, there are the cultural processes: movements, trends and ideas. These processes are not static but dynamic. For example, the cultural process that occurred in San Francisco during the 1960's and early 70's with the Hippies and the development of a counter-culture is no longer happening there today. If you go to Haight-Asbury today in search of Hippies you won't find them; the process has moved on.

Then there are the political processes. There are some cities that are centers for political power and strength, like Moscow, London, or Washington DC. They have influence on the world today, but that's not to say they will still have influence 50 years from now.

There are also economic processes. Cities are centers for industry and trade, and the majority of city dwellers are involved in some way or another in this process. Some cities, such as Los Angeles, have become extremely wealthy. In 1986, greater Los Angeles produced $250 billion worth of goods and services, making the 12.6 million people in the metropolitan area the world's eleventh largest "nation" in terms of gross national product, ahead of Australia, India, and Switzerland. Tokyo is another city influencing the economics of the world. Decisions made in board rooms of Tokyo affect not only Japan, but the rest of the world.

Lastly, there are spiritual processes. Each city has its spiritual dynamics, but the spiritual life of some cities, the Vatican City and Mecca being notable examples, reach far beyond their geographic location.

That these four processes come together in the city, and the sheer numbers of people who now live in urbanized areas, should say something about the seriousness of going into the city. The city is fast becoming the reality of life for the majority of the world's population, especially in the developing world. By the year 2000 New York and Los Angeles will be the only western cities figuring among the world's fourteen largest cities.

Cities are places of tremendous need. The statistics we have been referring to and the processes we have elaborated on involve people. As the demographics and processes of a city change they have a direct affect on people. If more people move into a geographic area than it can adequately support you get the slums and squatter communities that have become the reality of life in many cities of the developing world.

The function of a city may also change. For example, many cities in the western world are shifting from labor-intensive to capital-intensive economies. With this movement comes tremendous pressure to the poor. There are no longer as many jobs available as there were, and the loss of job opportunities coupled with rapid urbanization is creating great tension for the working class.

In the developing world many nations are rushing to create industrial infrastructures to keep pace with the west at the cost of giving up their agriculturally based economies. People flock to the cities in search of a better life, only to find there is not enough work for all those who seek it. In Manila over half the city's population of 10 to 12 million people are either unemployed, or under-employed selling cigarettes, papers or flowers to passing motorists and tourists.

As the representatives of Jesus Christ on this earth, we must respond to the city and its needs. In ignoring the city, the church is ignoring the heart-cry of humanity. I believe God is saying to the church, "Go to the city." We must respond to that call. We must pray and intercede and ask God for appropriate ways to reach the city.

Cities have influences that go far beyond their geographic location, and we need to turn that influence into influence for good. Think of Los Angeles and the tremendous impact the city has worldwide through arts and entertainment. Think of New York and London and the impact they have on the world through their financial institutions. Think of Tokyo and the tremendous influence it has on technology and business. It is time for the church not only to reach the people of the city, but also to get involved in the life of the city and turn it around for good. Jeremiah 29:7 tells us, "Seek the welfare of the city where I have sent you . . .for in its welfare you will have welfare." We cannot afford to abandon the city. What shows up in the city today, be it fashion, technological breakthrough, medical discovery, or the latest religious cult, will arrive tomorrow in small towns.

Each city should be approached with a unique strategy that fits the personality of the city and the culture of the people we are ministering to. No one strategy can adequately respond to all the needs of the city. The strategies that are effective in bringing Hispanics to the Lord in Los Angeles will not work on the city's Vietnamese population. We must seek God for effective strategies for reaching each particular people group within the urban environment.

God is shaking up the world. He is bringing the world to our doorstep. While God is bringing the peoples of the world to us in our great cities, many of us are fleeing the city, preoccupied with our own security and happiness. We want to escape the danger of urban ghettos and the "corrupting" influence of the big city, and settle in "safe" suburbs. But in those safe suburbs, we slowly drift into a deadened sense of spirituality and a compromised commitment to Christ.

We must awaken to God's plan for our lives by repenting of our self-centeredness. Suburbs can corrupt our children just as fast as cities. Suburban kids are just as sinful as inner-city kids. The safest place in this world is in God's will. If we have values that blind us to God's call upon our lives, we must cast them off and seek God's Kingdom first. We are in a spiritual battle. Satan is lying to God's people by trying to appease them with comfort and prosperity, while hundreds of millions of people suffer in physical need and die without the knowledge of Christ.

You will never find fulfilment by running from God. He created you to live for Him and for others, not for yourself. Put God first. Then, and only then, will you discover the secret to fulfilment and happiness. Security is not found in the countryside, it is found in Christ!

Christ is in the city. Celebrate Christ in the city. Discover Christ in the city. It is His dwelling place.

Chapter Seven

Children – The Small Half Of The World

Floyd McClung

The children of our world are being robbed; they're being robbed of their childhood innocence. Across the globe children are having to cope with physical and emotional stresses that children were never supposed to bear. As a result, they are physically, emotionally, psychologically, and spiritually adrift.

We in the church must take seriously the plight of children in our world. 35% of the world's 5 billion inhabitants are under 15 years, and 50% are under the age of 25. Our world is a young world, especially the developing world where 45% of all Africans, 37% of all Asians, and 38% of all Latin Americans are under 15. The future of our world lies in the future of its children. Today's children will morally and spiritually shape tomorrow's societies.

In the developing world, the ravages of famine and poverty have placed the battle to survive squarely on the shoulders of children. Destitute and desperately poor parents are forced to leave their children to their own devices. 10,000 children a day die in the developing world from diseases that could have been easily prevented with immunization. Another 40,000 children under the age of five die daily from malnutrition. 200 million have no access to clean drinking water which in turn perpetuates the cycle of disease.

There are 80 million homeless children living on city streets of the developing world. According to *Time Magazine*, 14 million of them are in Brazil. In Belo Horizonte, Brazil, where a Youth With A Mission team is working, there are 300,000 homeless children living in the streets in a city whose entire population is a little less than two million people. Children caught in these tragic circumstances are left with lasting physical, and spiritual damage.

Many children in the world have been emotionally scarred by forced and premature adulthood. They have watched helplessly as family members die of malnutrition and other diseases. They have experienced blood-chilling violence and brutality wrought by invading armies or rebel forces. Violence for many has become a daily reality. One young Cambodian refugee whose family was killed by the Pol Pot regime, and whose legs were blown off by a landmine, said, "Sometimes I'm okay and sometimes I'm not okay. Sometimes I remember things. Every day I am depressed a little."

Children of the developing world are also suffering at the hands of a sinister child trade. A December 1987 article in South Magazine documented how poverty has turned children into commodities to be bought and sold. While the buying and selling of children is illegal in almost all nations, the debt-ridden governments of the developing world are adept at turning a blind eye. The need for foreign currency and corruption have helped this flourishing business. Babies are bought from impoverished mothers by middlemen who pay between US$40-60. These babies are in turn sold to adoption agencies who pay several thousand dollars each for them. Not only are babies being bought and sold, but young children as well. Many children are sold into prostitution, pornography, or child labor rings.

Currently there are 145 million children who are part of the labor force. Most of them are forced to work as virtual slaves for up to eighteen hours a day in dingy sweatshops. They are exposed to the danger of unsafe machinery, poisonous fumes, and poor lighting and ventilation. In one confectionery factory raided in Thailand by police, they found two young children who had died, and others who were too weak even to walk.

The demand for child pornography has created an almost insatiable need for children to be used in its production. This, in addition to the demand for child prostitutes, has lead to the enslavement of millions of children in the sex business. This situation is not confined to children in the developing world: many of the runaways in the developed world also end up ensnared in prostitution or pornography.

Children of the developed world are facing situations that a generation ago were adult problems. Pre-teenagers are having to grapple with the emotional stress of sexual immorality, drug and alcohol abuse, the dislocation and disintegration of the family, and manipulation at the hands of the media.

An epidemic of teenage suicide is sweeping the developed world. Over 6,000 teenagers last year committed suicide in the United States. 71% of teenagers who attempt suicide are from broken homes. One study conducted among teenagers from broken homes found that 75% of them felt guilty and responsible for the break-up of their parents. Other factors leading to teenage suicide are substance abuse and sexual involvement. Younger and younger children are becoming sexually involved, and when these relationships break up, they are unable to deal with the resulting emotional trauma.

Along with greater sexual involvement has come an explosion in teenage pregnancy. The United States currently has the developed world's highest teenage pregnancy rate, with over one million teenage girls, some as young as eleven, twelve and thirteen getting pregnant every year. Some 400,000 of these pregnancies end in abortion, leaving deep emotional scars.

Through television, movies, and music, children are bombarded with an endless stream of consumer appeals. Moreover, sexual immorality, drug abuse, and violence are all presented as completely acceptable behavior for today's youth. Rarely, however, do they see the unglamorous, dehumanizing results of such behavior

The advertisements that run during children's programming on television are slick appeals designed to create desires young children find hard to resist. They portray to children the notion that to be really accepted by others they need name-brand products or kiddies' designer clothes. Suddenly children can no longer be children and have a regular doll. Instead, it has to be a talking, crying, wetting doll, sold at inflated prices by greedy manufacturers who prey on the susceptibility of children.

Such attacks on our children must not go unheeded. Satan has declared war on a whole generation. The churches greatest weapon in response to this onslaught is not only a strengthened family, but to believe in its youth and to enlist them in the cause of world evangelization.

The future, as well as the present welfare of the church, lies in the hands of the youth of the world. The future missionaries, Bible teachers, and Christian leaders are now emerging. Let's enlist them in world evangelization! Don't wait until they are 25 or 30 years old. Just as a relay runner calls out to the next runner to "go" as he prepares to hand him the baton, so we must call upon our youth to be involved now, to lead now. We must prepare for the future by opening up doors of opportunity in the present. Failure to do this may compromise the future effectiveness and vibrancy of the church.

We must elevate the status of children's ministries in the church. We must see ministry to children as more than running Sunday School or Saturday night youth programs. Yes, we need these programs, but we must invite them to take a lead in evangelizing their own generation, Evangelizing the children of the world must become a priority.

We must develop new strategies and new approaches for evangelizing the youth of the world. Our world is a rapidly changing place and the strategies used a decade ago will not work today. Our strategies must be up-to-date and relevant; otherwise, they will fail to communicate effectively the vital message we want to share.

Today's youth are interested in spiritual things. The problem is that they are not attracted by the forms or programs we have been using. A recent study conducted among teenagers in Amsterdam found that 96% of those questioned were interested in religion, God, or reading the Bible. The same study also found that 100% of those questioned had an interest in music. Such statistics should suggest something about the forms evangelism and church life should take.

There are many teenagers on the streets in Amsterdam and music has been one of the keys to reaching them with the gospel. A young man from Youth With A Mission formed a band called "No Longer Music", and the band is having an impact in Amsterdam. Many young people are coming to know the Lord. This band has been successful because they have found a form through which they can present the gospel to people who would otherwise never grace the door of a church to hear the gospel.

Our strategies for evangelizing the youth of the world must also include the developing world. We must address the plight of developing world children. Not only must we share the gospel with them, but we must deal with the injustice that ensnares and emotionally wounds these children. We must deal with the problems of starvation and famine. We must provide educational opportunities. We must give love and emotional support. The need among the children of the developing world is too great for us too ignore.

As the church, we must also re-affirm the value of the family everywhere we go. The break-up of the family, both in the developing and developed world, is having a devastating effect on our children. We must respond to this crisis with more than just warnings about the evils of divorce. We must provide support and counsel when the family is faced with difficulty and stress. Where the family has already suffered irreparable damage, we, the church, must step in as surrogate parents. We must provide an atmosphere where children and teenagers feel loved, affirmed, needed, and appreciated. We must supply the self-esteem and sense of value and importance these children need. Otherwise, they will turn to other things in trying to deal with the emptiness, hurt and frustration they are feeling.

I believe the church must also be preparing to pass the baton of leadership to the youth of the world. In a relay race no single runner runs the whole distance. Rather, a number of runners each take their turn at running a part of the distance. As a new runner gets ready for his part in the race he begins jogging, arm outstretched, waiting for the other runner to pass the baton to him. Once he has received the baton he gives the race his all until it is his turn to pass the baton to another runner. Notice, before the runner receives the baton he is already in motion. It is time to pass the baton of leadership on to the youth of the church that they might bring their youthful enthusiasm, joy, excitement, and energy to bear on the task of evangelism and the affairs of the church. We must not just be running youth programs in the church; we must be seeking to integrate youth into all aspects of church life. We must be setting them in motion, readying them to receive the baton. We must be releasing responsibility and ministry to them so that they might do their part toward completing the great commission. With the children goes the future. We must make sure that future is world evangelization.

Chapter Eight

The World Of Islam

Kalafi Moala

Speak of Islam and to our mind comes the images of a garbed, bearded Ayatollah with piercing cold steel eyes. Of fanatical young people decrying the west as they load themselves on to buses that will deliver them to a war zone and almost certain death. Of women in black chadors, only their eyes showing above the veil. We hear of the terrorism and violence that issues from the Middle East and we wonder, what is this thing called Islam?

Islam is an all-encompassing way of life. Literally translated, "Islam" means "Submission to the will of God". Unlike Christians, who see submission in terms of a child submitting to his father, Muslims see themselves as slaves of Allah. In whatever circumstance they find themselves in this life it is Allah's will and they must accept it. As a result, Muslims can be fatalistic in their view of life. Islam teaches that there is one God and Mohammed was his greatest prophet. A Muslim is taught that he has two angels watching over him. One to record his bad deeds, and the other to record his good deeds. On the Day of Judgement every Muslim man's deeds will be weighed. If the good deeds outweigh the bad then he will enjoy life in paradise. However, if the bad outweighs the good he will endure an eternity of suffering and torture at the hands of Satan. Redemption in Islam rests squarely with the individual.

Islam is one of the world's fastest growing religions with nearly one billion adherents. One out of every five people on earth is a Muslim. The Islamic world stretches across North Africa, Asia and Europe and includes not only such countries as, Saudi Arabia, Iran, Turkey, Syria, and Libya, but also countries such as the Soviet Union, India, China and Indonesia. Indeed, Asia has the four largest Muslim countries in the world, Indonesia, India, Pakistan, and Bangledesh, with the Soviet Union being the fifth largest.

Islam is also the fastest growing religion in Europe. In 1949 the first mosque in the Netherlands began operation, and today there are over 200 Islamic places of worship. Muslims account for 2.1% of the Dutch population. In Germany there are an estimated 1.9 million Muslims. A large part of the growth in Europe is due to immigration from Muslim nations, but in the spiritual vacuum of Europe an increasing number of Europeans are converting to Islam, particularly women who marry Muslim men. Recently the Libyan-based Society for the Preaching and Spreading of Islam opened in Bonn, West Germany. The aim of this organization, which has an annual budget of $100 million, is to promote the building of Islamic cultural centers and training establishments in the West. Islam is also on the increase in Southern Africa. Kuwait has taken on the responsibility of saturating the nation of Malawi with Islam and establishing mosques. It is their intention to cover the nation with mosques built 20 kilometers apart in every direction. Saudi Arabia has likewise taken on a similar project in Zambia. Throughout the world, Islam is on the move.

Despite the geographic and demographic size of the Islamic world, and despite the zealousness with which Muslims are seeking to propagate their faith worldwide, there are only 2000 Christian missionaries working among them. How can this be? Why has the church invested so little of its resource in this vast mission field?

I believe there are several reasons why we haven't pursued reaching the Muslim. First, Christians in general have been hard-hearted in their attitude toward Muslims. They have not loved Muslims and obeyed the Lord's command to reach them. Muslims may be hard to reach, but we have not tried enough, for there are many who are open to the gospel. Muslims can be resistent to the gospel. Islam for them is more than just a religion; it is the sum total of their cultural heritage. They perceive that to become a Christian is to deny that heritage and become a traitor to one's country. In many cases, for a Muslim to become a Christian means certain and complete separation from family and friends. Such rejection is not easy to bear, especially since there are virtually no Christian churches that can help fill the void such rejection leaves.

Most Muslims also feel Christianity has nothing to offer them. Indeed, as they look back through their history, they find that Christianity has all too often meant bad news for them. They look to the "Crusades" that left tens of thousands of Muslims dead as the "Holy Land" was reclaimed for Christians. They look to the more recent past and their treatment at the hands of often ruthless "Christian" colonial powers. And they look to the state of today's so-called Christian nations. As one Muslim man asked, "If America is a Christian nation, then why does the worst filth in the world pour out of it around the globe?"

Because of this resistance to the gospel, the church has become apathetic in its attitude toward the Muslin world. We would sooner use our resources in places where the going is easier and the results more dramatic. The western world has become such a result-oriented society that we are not willing to make the commitment of time and resources to something that may take years before any appreciable results are seen.

I believe fear and unbelief rules the church in relation to the Muslim world. We have seen how hard this mission field is, we have seen the images of the Muslim world that the media passes before us, and it has caused fear and unbelief to take root in our heart. Deep down in our hearts we wonder if it's really possible to reach the Muslim world with the gospel.

We must repent of such belief. Yes, over 80% of all Muslims have never heard of the gospel. Yet, it has been a hard mission field. Yes, there is sometimes the threat of bodily harm. But we must never lose sight of the fact that Muslims are people with the same needs and feelings as we have, and Jesus died for them as much as He died for us. God is infinitely bigger than any problem or hardship we may encounter in reaching the Muslim world.

I believe that victory in reaching the Muslim world is primarily won on our knees in prayer. We need to be interceding and crying out to God for the Muslim world. We need to be asking Him for new strategies in reaching out to this area. We also need to be asking Him for more workers for the Muslim world. Prayer is a two-edged sword because, should He tell us to go in answer to our prayer, will we be willing to go? I believe God wants to reap a great harvest among Muslims in the decade ahead. However, that harvest starts with us getting on our knees, repenting of our unbelief and getting serious about reaching the Muslim world with the gospel.

I believe God is going to release thousands of workers into this harvest field. There will be people dedicated to the task of breaking the fetters of Islam and bringing the light of the gospel regardless of how long it takes and what it costs. These workers need to be trained and have a good understanding of Muslim culture and Muslim peoples. They may need to be tent-making missionaries, working at a job while at the same time reaching Muslims with the gospel. They also need to be workers who know and rely upon the supernatural power of God.

God loves Muslims, and we must begin targeting them with the Gospel. Not only the large Muslim countries, but also the small ones such as Brunei, the Maldives, and the Malay people of Malaysia and Singapore. It is time to go to the Muslim world with the gospel. The harvest is great and God will deliver it into our hands. Currently, the greatest response to the gospel among Muslims is in Indonesia, where, on the island of Java, literally thousands have become Christians. God is wanting to do the same thing in other Muslim countries. God loves Muslims – do we?

Chapter Nine

The Buddhist World

Kalafi Moala

During the 5th century B.C., a prince and heir to the throne of a small principality in Northern India left his wife and child in the middle of the night and became a wandering ascetic in search of the truth. After six years of rigorous asceticism he still had not found the truth he sought, until one night as he meditated under a Bodhi tree he began to understand the essential nature of the universe, and by dawn he had become the "Enlightened One", the Buddha.

Buddhism is an outgrowth of an early form of Hinduism, and shares with Hinduism a belief in the law of Karma and reincarnation. Karma is the debit balance of good and evil actions that is carried forward from one existence to another (reincarnation). Gautama Buddha is reputed to have passed through 10,000 incarnations before achieving enlightenment. In Buddhism the ultimate liberation from the cycle of birth, death, and rebirth is called "Nirvana".

Buddhism's growth was slow at first, but during the twelfth century a Buddhist revival occurred in Ceylon (Sri Lanka). News of the revival spread and soon monks from the Mon, Thai, and Khmer peoples went to Ceylon and studied the newly revised Buddhist scriptures. They brought what they had learned home with them and combined it with their existing animistic and Brahmanistic practices. Gradually Buddhism took hold as the predominant religion of Southeast Asia.

Today Buddhism has 315 million adherents and encompasses China, Tibet, Vietnam, Cambodia, Laos, Thailand, Burma, Malaysia, Korea, Japan, Taiwan, Sri Lanka, Bhutan, and India. It is a large and diverse mission field, and much of it is restricted in access.

The Buddhist world is a hard, unyielding mission field that is very resistant to the gospel. Buddhism permeates all levels of culture and national identity, so to deny Buddhism is to deny one's national identity. But in the last 25 years, there have been remarkable spiritual break-throughs in many Buddhist lands. During 1972 the Spirit of God moved in Cambodia and many thousands of people heard and responded to the gospel, but this move was cut short in 1975 by the coming-to-power of Pol Pot's communist government.

Indeed, war and its aftermath has interrupted what Christian missionary work had been done in Vietnam, Cambodia, and Laos. With communist governments now firmly ensconced, these countries are closed to missionaries. Other places such as Tibet and Bhutan are isolated and hard to reach.

Despite the apparent hardships, some exciting things have been happening. Since 1982 a worker with Campus Crusade for Christ in northern Thailand has established 720 churches among Buddhist people. Independent of this move of God in Northern Thailand, Dr. Kriengsak Chareonwongsak, a university professor, began a church in Bangkok that has experienced remarkable growth. The Hope of Bangkok Church is the fastest growing church in the city. It started as a Bible study of five people in 1980, and now has over 3000 people attending its services, and runs 300 cell group meetings weekly. The Hope of Bangkok church has a goal of establishing a local church in every province of Thailand by the year 2000.

Seventy-five years of missionary work produced approximately 5000 to 10,000 converts in Cambodia. However, in the first few months of the exodus of refugees from Cambodia to the refugee camps of Thailand, some 30,000 Khmer Buddhists became Christians, and that number has continued to grow steadily. Several teams have recently been in Tibet where they are laying the foundations for a thrust of evangelism into the nation.

Korea is another example of what God wants to do in the Buddhist world. Forty years ago Korea was a Buddhist nation. Today, it is on its way to becoming a Christian nation. A quarter of its population is now Christian, and that figure is added to annually by a million new Korean converts. Seoul, Korea has become the city of mega-churches, boasting the largest Pentecostal, United Methodist, Presbyterian, and soon Baptist churches in the world.

God is going to do mighty things in the Buddhist world, and He wants us, His church, to participate with Him in it. If we will rise up and take the opportunities that exist, God will go before us. We need to start targeting nations in the Buddhist world for prayer and evangelism, nations such as Bhutan, where there are only about 3000 known Christians in a total population of 2.4 million people, or Sikkim, the tiny Indian state located between Bhutan and Nepal, which is almost totally unevangelized. If we will do our part, God will work with us in seeing the Buddhist world evangelized.

Chapter Ten

The Hindu World

Kalafi Moala

According to tradition, the Apostle Thomas was the first to preach the gospel in India. He arrived in southern India in A.D. 52 and set about winning to the Lord members of the Brahmin, or upper caste, and Jews who also lived in the area. Thomas' arrival signaled the start of a long history of Christian missions in India. Yet, despite the effort of two thousand years, today only about 18 million people, or 3% of India's population, claim to be Christians, and approximately three quarters of these Christians live in southern India.

While Hinduism is predominantly confined to the Indian sub-continent, (83% of India's nearly 800 million inhabitants are Hindu), emigration and the export of Indian labor during the colonial days have left enclaves of Hinduism around the world. Most notable is the South Pacific nation of Fiji where over 40% of the population are Hindus, and Bali, Indonesia, whose population of three million is predominantly Hindu. The more philosophical and mystical sides of Hinduism have also gained popularity in the western world, where Transcendental Meditation and "Spiritual Enlightenment" seminars run by various Hindu Gurus and holy men are now common, and where saffron-robed devotees chanting and ringing bells on street corners are now part of the landscape of most cities. The Hindu world also encompasses Nepal, the small Himalayan nation squeezed between India to the south and Tibet and China to the north. Nepal is the only country in the world where Hinduism is the official religion. 90% of Nepal's 18 million people are Hindu.

As it has done for so many centuries, the Hindu world presents the church with a formidable challenge in the area of evangelism. Hindus have remained largely resilient to the gospel, and in the case of Nepal, it is against the law to convert from Hinduism to any other religion. Indeed, Christians in Nepal are openly persecuted. Despite this, the Nepalese church is experiencing growth and there are now between 20 to 30 thousand Christians in Nepal.

The Hindu world also presents the church with a formidable challenge in the area of human need. Hinduism is a fatalistic religion that is oblivious to the needs of other human beings. So, while some 200 to 300 million holy cows roam the land devouring whatever they may, people die of starvation. The social structure of the Hindu faith also allows people of a higher caste to indifferently stand by as those of lower castes suffer and die of hunger and disease. Cities such as Calcutta and Bombay have huge "basti's" or slums where millions of people perch precariously on the verge of starvation.

In Calcutta, 80% of the city's 11 million people live in one-room apartments, and 300,000 people sleep on the sidewalks. Beggars in Calcutta sit, despairing and weak, waiting for death to overtake them, while in Bombay the average slum dweller is 4 inches shorter than other Indian men because of malnutrition. 50% of the children in Bombay die before they are four years old.

The need in Hindu India is great and the church must respond. An army of evangelists is needed. One of our mission leaders in India recently told me that if we were to put a thousand teams on the Indian sub-continent, and each week each team went to a new village where the gospel had not been preached before and where there was no church, those thousand teams could travel for ten years and never encounter one another. There are about 600,000 villages in India, most untouched by the gospel. Not only must we win people to the Lord, but we also respond to the enormous physical need. We must bring healing for the whole man, body, soul, and spirit.

As mentioned earlier, there are also pockets of Hinduism spread across the globe. We must respond with the gospel to the Hindu populations of Fiji, Bali, and the cities of the world. Though Hindus are rarely won by argumentation, they are deeply impressed with love and friendship.

Chapter Eleven

The World Of Tribal Peoples

Kalafi Moala

Until a decade ago the Zuruaha people had never had contact with anyone from the outside world. Life for them consisted of hunting with blow-pipes and poison-tipped arrows, and when wild pigs and monkeys were scarce they would migrate to another settlement further into the jungle. No one had seen or had contact with these people, except for riverboat operators, who from time to time had seen Zuruaha men crouching in the shadows along the river-bank.

From the river-boat operators a young Brazilian woman, Braulia, heard of the existence of the Zuruaha people. She began praying for these people and eventually convinced a local settler to guide her and her two companions to the Zuruaha's camp. They made contact with the Zuruaha, who were intrigued by them, and set about the task of learning their language and translating the gospel.

Things were not easy for Braulia. Her two companions took sick and had to return down the river, and at times she felt more like a slave to the tribe than a missionary. However, through prayer she persevered and began to notice the attitude of the tribespeople changing toward her. Soon she was welcomed into the tribe. The tribe's women took her to a nearby stream and there ceremoniously bathed her and gave her the clothes of a Zuruaha woman to wear. Dancing and songs followed, after which she was given a Zuruaha name.

As a result of Braulia's faith and persistence she was able to penetrate the Zuruaha people and share the gospel with them. People who believed in the spirits of the trees, rocks and rivers, for the first time heard of Jesus and His love for them, and began to believe.

The Zuruaha live in the Amazon basin, but there are tribal groups on every continent, and many of them, because of their unique language and customs, remain outside the reach of the gospel. In North America, the Zuni and Hopi peoples of the Southwest remain among the most unreached tribal peoples on earth. Mexico has over 400 unreached tribal groups, and in the Amazon Basin there are dozens of groups who have had no contact with the outside world at all. In the Chittagong Hill Tracts of Bangladesh, the Chakmas, the Mogs and the Tripuraies remain some of the most unreached and restricted-access tribal peoples in the world. There are also many unreached tribal groups in Irian Jaya, Indonesia, Burma, Thailand and in other areas of Asia.

Despite the great cultural distance that exists between these tribes and much of the church, tribal peoples are some of the most responsive to the gospel. Most of the tribes of Nagaland, India, for example, have turned to Christ and have become active in sending missionaries to other parts of India and beyond. Through the ministry of such groups as Wycliffe Bible Translators and New Tribes Missions, hundreds of other tribal peoples have heard the gospel and been able to escape from the web of demonic fear that ensnared them. Yet there are still many thousands of tribal peoples that are unreached with the gospel.

Sharing the gospel among tribal peoples requires long-term commitment, since it takes time to learn the language of the tribe and adapt to their customs. Often a missionary has to rely on non-literate forms of communication, such as stories and drama, to communicate the message of the gospel. The close kinship structure of tribal societies and their fear of other tribes has caused large missionary teams to be unsuccessful. Instead, one or two missionaries must deal alone with isolation, loneliness, and illness as they penetrate a tribe with the gospel.

For these reasons many western Christians view ministry among tribal peoples with reserve or disdain, seeing work among such small groups of people as insignificant and not worth the effort. They forget, however, that 2000 years ago much of Northern and Central Europe was inhabited by such "tribal" groups as the Celts, Franks, and Vikings. Roaming from region to region, these groups often had such customs as drinking from human skulls and consulting with shaman before venturing out to gather food or make war.

In the first century after Christ many of the tribes living near the Mediterranean were reached with the gospel. In turn these tribes shared the gospel with other tribal people groups and slowly the gospel began to spread across Central Europe and into the British Isles. In later centuries, Irish monks walked barefooted into the forests of Northern Europe and reached isolated Germanic tribes, teaching them the creeds and establishing churches. Viking groups in Scandinavia were won to Christ largely by the British and Irish Christians kidnapped during the many Viking raids on the British Isles.

Over time these "tribes", the Franks, Gauls, and Anglo-Saxons, have gone on to people such places as France, Germany, Great Britain, Sweden, and even the United States. With this in mind, western Christians need to humbly take up the challenge of reaching unreached tribal groups with the gospel.

Scripture tells us that around the Throne of God there will be people from "every nation, tribe, people and language". For this to be a reality, the church must mobilize and go to every unreached tribal group with the gospel, even those in remote or inaccessible regions of the world.

Perhaps the Lord has a tribe prepared for you, and your obedience in going to them will mean they hear the gospel for the first time!

Chapter Twelve

Nominal Christians
Of The World

Floyd McClung

"We must evangelize those who are already baptized." So said Pope John Paul II at the 1982 Bishop's Synod in Rome in reference to the Roman Catholic Church. The same statement could also apply to any number of Protestant denominations. An estimated 1.3 billion people in the world claim to be affiliated to a Christian denomination. This is not to say they all go to church. In Finland 94% of the population consider themselves to be Lutherans, but only 5% of them attend church on a regular basis, and less than 1% take Communion. Such figures illustrate that a large pool of people consider themselves Christians only in the broadest sense of the word.

The Lausanne Committee for World Evangelization defines a nominal Christian as "one who would call himself a Christian, or be so regarded by others, but who has no authentic commitment to Christ based on personal faith." Furthermore, nominal Christians can be divided into two categories, those who attend church, either regularly or occasionally, but have no personal relationship with Jesus, and those who do not attend church, and may even be antagonistic toward traditional Christianity, but consider themselves Christians by virtue of their birth, or country of residence.

I believe, in our effort to complete the great commission, we must also concentrate on evangelizing nominal Christians. Our strategies for evangelizing this group must take into account the two categories noted above. We must develop strategies for reaching out to both those who are more closely connected to a local church or parish, and to those who have no connection whatsoever.

Our emphasis in reaching the first group must be on helping them to make Jesus Lord of their lives. We must show them that being a Christian involves more than just involvement in, and adherence to, the teaching of a particular denomination or confession. Such things are important, but we only become committed Christians by making Jesus Lord of our lives. For this group, we also need to establish Bible study, prayer, and discipleship groups that can nurture and disciple them after they have committed themselves to Jesus Christ. Perhaps we could call these structures "wineskins within wineskins." These structures provide support, encouragement and discipleship for a person, without him ever having to forsake his own denomination or church. We do need to establish alternative services, but not on Sunday mornings, in order to form such "nurture" structures within the traditional church.

Evangelism amongst nominal Christians is for the purpose of helping them know Christ personally and to grow in their faith. In turn we want to teach them to lead others within their denomination into a relationship with Christ. We want them to bring a spirit of renewal and revival to their denomination.

For too long, evangelism of nominal Christians has been done in a confrontational mode. Our evangelism has often consisted of trying to convince them of what is wrong with their denomination or confession of belief. It is time to stop confusing evangelism and evangelicalism. Though it may seem a bit ridiculous to some, it is important for believers to form an open attitude toward the church background to realize that one can be both a committed Christian and a Lutheran or Anglican. Becoming a committed Christian means acceptance of Christ and all He has done for us, but does not mean we must accept all that is taught in a church.

There is no perfect church. People can look at our church and find as many faults in it as we can in theirs. We must draw alongside nominal Christians, love them, accept them, and demonstrate what a relationship with God is really like. We must show them that simply calling ourselves Christian and claiming allegiance to a certain confession of faith does not automatically give us a relationship with Jesus. We must demonstrate that God can be known in an intimate way.

Reaching the non-church-attending nominal Christian requires quite a different approach. Indeed the strategies required here fall fairly into the existing strategies of evangelism employed by many churches. Because these people do not attend church, and may even be antagonistic to their Christian upbringing, one cannot presume a person will believe in God or see his need of Christ.

Of all the "worlds" around us, perhaps none is easier for the majority of Christians to get involved in than evangelizing nominal Christians. We live in neighbourhoods, towns and cities where thousands of nominal Christians also live. Perhaps our next door neighbours are nominal Christians. Are we concerned about their spiritual well-being? Each member of Christ's church is called to be an evangelist. It is time to become what He expects us to be and begin reaping a great harvest of souls in this mission field that is literally on our doorstep.

Chapter Thirteen

The Communist World

Floyd McClung

It is time to emphasize evangelism in the Communist world.

It is time we broadened our perspective in the church about the ministry in Communist countries. We have concentrated much on the suffering church and smuggling Bibles into these countries, but every day in these same countries thousands of people die without knowing Christ. The time has come for aggressive evangelism in the Communist world. In saying this, I do not mean to belittle the plight of Christians in these lands, or imply that there is no need for Bibles and Christian literature. There is, and many ministries are fulfilling a vital role in providing support and materials for these Christians. What I do mean to imply is that we cannot focus solely on the suffering church and smuggling Bibles as our ministry to the Communist world.

The great commission is not premised upon whether people live in accessible parts of the world, or whether they live in Communist or non-Communist nations. Jesus said to go into all the world, and that is what we must do whether the country be China, the Soviet Union, or any other nation. Our decision whether or not to minister in a country cannot be based on the kind of government it has, or whether it is legal to share the gospel. Our decision must be based on whether or not there are people in that country who need to hear the gospel. Our mandate to preach the gospel comes from the King who is above all governments and earthly powers.

I am not trying to make a case for outright civil disobedience, but I am trying to make the case for boldness in evangelism that is motivated by the needs of the lost. We need an army of evangelists who will carry the gospel into the Communist world. Many doors are open to do this through cultural exchange programs, studying in universities, and through business and travel.

In Acts chapter 26 the Apostle Paul is brought from prison to give a defense before King Agrippa and Festus, the Roman governor of Palestine. These two men held Paul's life in the balance. Paul, however, was not intimidated by them and, instead, boldly gave his testimony and presented the gospel. Festus told Paul he was mad (verse 24), but King Agrippa said, "You almost persuade me to become a Christian" (verse 28). Paul had spoken with such passion and boldness that he almost convinced one of the men adjudging his case to believe. Evangelism today needs to be immersed in this kind of boldness. Our lives are in the hands of God and we should not be intimidated by anyone who thinks otherwise.

In the western world we have many misconceptions about countries behind the Iron and Bamboo Curtains. Our media has taught us to look at them as the enemy, as ruthless "evil empires". Many of the things said about various Communist countries in the media may be true, but as Christians we must view these countries as Jesus views them – as people He loves and longs to touch and fill with His new life. He died for these people as much as He died for people in the free world.

Contrary to popular belief, the 1.7 billion people who inhabit the Communist world are not all doctrinaire, card-carrying, Marxists. They are people like you and me, with the same hopes, fears, dreams, ambitions, feelings and needs, and one of those needs is spiritual – they need to hear of a God who loves and cares for them.

In many of these countries there is much openness to the gospel. A friend of mine recently related to me the experience of his first visit to China. He was with several others on the trip and one day they decided to walk through a market. They took with them a bag containing several hundred Chinese tracts which they hoped to be able to distribute. There were a number of people in the market, so, apprehensively, they opened their bag and took out handfuls of the tracts. "I have handed out many thousands of tracts before," my friend said, "but never have I seen a response like the response of these Chinese people. As we began handing out the tracts people came running from everywhere to get one, and the scene soon looked like a riot as people climbed over each other to get a tract." He also told me how, as they were distributing the tracts, he looked across the crowd and to his dismay saw a guard making his way toward them. But, to his relief and surprise, the guard looked at what they were doing, then took one of the tracts and walked off reading it. In just a few minutes in the market they gave away every tract they had with them to people who were eager to receive.

As many evangelism teams from Youth With A Mission have gone into other Communist countries they too have found a similar openness and hunger to know more about the gospel.

When Communist governments have tried to stamp out religion, they have not prevailed. In the case of China their efforts had the opposite effect. After the last missionaries were forced out of China in the early 1950's, they left behind an estimated 700,000 Christians. As the Chinese church suffered through the ravages of the Cultural Revolution, many in the west believed it could not survive. Pastors were torn from their congregations and tortured and imprisoned. Churches were closed. Bibles were banned and confiscated.

Christians were harshly persecuted and because of their faith, they were separated and sent in a thousand different directions. Christians were scattered over the vast matum of China. In one fell swoop, the government of Red China became the largest missions board in the world, sending tens if not hundreds of thousands of Chinese Christians to every part of the land. As a result, the church grew and by the end of the Cultural Revolution, instead of there being no church left in China, there were an estimated 30 to 50 million Christians!

This raises a problem that is part and parcel of fulfilling the great commission – discipling and establishing converts in church fellowships. Persecution has left many church groups without proper leadership to follow up all those who make decisions for Christ. The western church can help here by providing two things, personnel and discipleship materials.

Youth With A Mission has recently begun establishing discipleship programs inside the Soviet Union, and it is our goal to have a thousand such programs in towns and cities across the Soviet Union and Eastern Europe in the next ten years. We want to evangelize, disciple, and train Soviet and Eastern European people who in turn can go and do the same for others.

Many think it is hard to get into Communist countries, but nothing could be further from the truth. If you apply for a missionary visa, you will certainly encounter difficulty! However, many Communist countries welcome western students and tourists. The new openness developing in the Soviet Union toward the west not only makes getting visas easier, it also provides more opportunities to meet and interact with Soviet people.

Go as a student or tourist, but at the same time be an evangelist. Talk to people, befriend people, build relationships with people through which you can share the gospel with them. Such friendship evangelism has proved to be the most effective form of evangelism in the western world and so, too, is it in the Communist world.

We must also be open to the Lord and ready to share the gospel in any other way He may lead. This is not to say we should be unwise, but we should be listening for the Spirit's leading and obeying Him. One team of Christians were in a park and felt the Lord wanted them to stand up and preach the gospel. They had no one to translate for them so asked a nearby soldier if he spoke English. He said he spoke a little so they asked if he would translate. Before the soldier realized what was happening he was translating the gospel for passers-by.

A friend told how he was standing in a railway station in China when an old Chinese lady came up and tapped him on the arm. "Are you a Christmas?" she asked. He was puzzled for a moment, then realized she wanted to know if he was a Christian and told her he was. The old woman asked him to preach the gospel and said she would translate. So, right there in the main concourse of the railway station, he preached the gospel with the Chinese woman translating. He preached for twenty minutes before a guard came and told him to stop.

Last summer we had one of our Youth With A Mission bands performing in Poland. In just one concert they saw 300 people publicly give their lives to Jesus Christ.

There are also ways of being involved in missions on a longer-term basis in the communist world. You can attend university in one of these countries. You can be a student and at the same time be an evangelist. In China there are opportunities for westerners to teach English in high schools and colleges. I once met a young American man on a train in China. This young man had been teaching English in a college in one province of China. He told me of the opportunities he had had to share the gospel among the students of the college. He told of their spiritual hunger and how in the evenings he would hold Bible studies in their dormitory. Many had come to know the Lord, and after a short break in Hong Kong he was going back to the college to teach some more and disciple those who had made decisions for Christ. The long-term opportunities for sharing the gospel in the Communist world are there, and as a church we must search them out. (Addresses are available at the end of this book.)

There are 115 Christian organizations carrying literature to the suffering church. It is now time we also had 115 organizations working in evangelizing the lost in the Communist world. To see the great commission completed in these nations, we need a wave of evangelism, an army of dedicated Christians, who will fearlessly go and take the gospel. It is time for evangelism in the Communist world, and anything less is a betrayal of the great commission. The church can no longer afford to be intimidated by the Communist world. The eternal destiny of millions of people is at stake.

Part Three

Practical Steps For Getting Involved

Chapter Fourteen

Getting The Most From Short-Term Missions

Floyd McClung

The advent of the jet age has also spawned the age of short-term missions. Instead of the six months it took the first missionaries to Hawaii to get there from Boston, today that same distance can be covered in ten hours by airplane. Virtually every area of the world is now accessible within twenty-four hours of leaving home. This, of course, has created great potential in the area of missions, as numbers of people can now go to the mission field for short periods of time and apply their skills to the task of completing the great commission.

There was a time when short-term missions were viewed with skepticism by those who knew the difficulties of learning another language and culture. They had visions of masses of unskilled young people flooding the mission field, and in their ignorance and inexperience undoing all that the long-term missionaries had accomplished. There were some initial problems, but overall it has been a very positive experience for both the long-term and the short-term missionaries. Short-term missions have now become an accepted part of the missionary endeavour, and many mission agencies now run some sort of short-term program. For those of you who undertake a short-term mission it can be a wonderful, profitable, and enriching experience.

There are four basic reasons why mission agencies run short-term mission programs. They are designed to give firsthand experience of another culture. Short-term opportunities also exist so you can see and experience what God is doing on the mission field today. You can apply your efforts and talents toward furthering the work of the gospel on the mission field. Lastly, you can see if the mission field is where God may be wanting you long-term.

Knowing the short-term outreach is being run with these objectives in mind, you can move on to better prepare yourself for it.

Prepare for another culture

If experiencing another culture is part of the short-term outreach, there are several things you need to consider in order to lessen the amount of "culture shock" you experience. While you may call it culture shock, what it should more properly be called is "people shock". People are what make up a culture, and what you are shocked at is how they live, and how differently they do things from the ways you are accustomed. One of the temptations you will immediately face is to compare the new culture with your own and draw negative conclusions. Food is an example of this tendency to compare. We watch a woman preparing an evening meal for her family consisting of chopped, fried pig liver, rice and comote. Instead of saying to ourselves, "That looks interesting, I wonder what it tastes like?" All too often we compare and say something like "How gross! These people aren't civilized. I'll never eat any of that while I'm here. I wish I were home where mom could fix me a pizza." This process of comparison, criticizing and withdrawal is not totally unexpected, but how you handle it determines whether or not you can meet the challenge of living in another culture.

To spend your days in American or western hotels looking for people who speak "our language" so you can spend time dreaming and reminiscing about home, or criticizing the way these "foreigners" do things spells failure. If you give in to this temptation, your sense of shock at how differently other people live will be heightened and the short-term outreach will become an endurance test instead of the learning experience it should be.

There are a number of things you can do to lessen the effects of culture shock and ensure you make the most of your cross-cultural experience:

a) *Do some advanced planning and research.* Find out all you can about the people and culture you will be visiting. Look for things about the culture that might interest you, things you may want to investigate further when you get there.

b) *Talk to people who have been on a short-term outreach to the same nation or people.* Ask them about their experience. Was it rewarding? If not, why not? How did they handle the different culture? Are there things they would do differently next time? Listen to their comments, learn from their mistakes, and be aware of attitudes that helped them. Find out the types of things you can expect to encounter and the best ways to handle them so you can get the most from the experience.

c) *See people as individuals.* There is a great tendency to see people from another culture, especially a culture vastly different from our own, as a mass of sameness. But they are not. People are unique and different. Cultures are made of "individual people". Concentrate on developing a relationship with one or two people while you are there. Talk to them, find out why they do things the way they do. Find out things about their culture, and look for insights that may help you more effectively share the gospel with them. Be a learner. Don't try to tell them the way things should be done, the way they are done in your culture! Listen and learn about the way they do things. Such an attitude will build bridges to the culture you are in and ensure you have an enriching and enjoyable cross-cultural experience,

d) *Take the necessary precautions prior to going.* Get all the shots you need, make sure you are in good health and reasonably fit. Nothing is more debilitating than getting sick while you are away. Find out from the agency you will be working with the requirements for working in this area. Be wise about what you eat and drink, though at the same time don't insult the people and culture you are in by refusing to try any of their food.

e) *Pray for the country you will be working in.* Ask God to give you His heart for the people. Ask Him to help you be a learner. Make up your mind that you will love the people with God's love, and let nothing deter you from that goal. Prayer for people will keep your heart safe. If something offends you, ask God to soften your heart so you can see the situation as He does.

Go with "open eyes"

To see what God is doing on the mission field you must go with "open eyes". You may not always see the significance of things that may be occurring. Talk to missionaries about what is happening in the nation spiritually. I remember talking to a missionary who had been in the Philippines for twenty-five years and he told me that in all his twenty-five years there he had never seen such openness to the gospel as there presently is. Had I not talked to this missionary I may well have missed the significance of what God was doing in that nation. So ask questions of missionaries and local believers. Attend different churches and try to assess what God is doing in the nation or people group, and what impact the gospel is having there.

Knowing what God is doing in a nation or city will better equip you to pray for missions and missionaries, as well as prepare you to share more effectively with our church when you get home.

Be a servant

To apply your effort and skill toward furthering the work of the gospel on the mission field, you will want to go with a willing and ready heart to serve wherever there is a need. You could end up doing any number of things from sharing the gospel with people on the streets or door-to-door, to construction, secretarial work, even helping with food preparation. The key for success and enjoyment here is having a servant's heart. You may have skills that would be better used undertaking another task, but what is important is that you, to the best of your abilities, do what you are asked to do. Your effort may not seem like much, or even very "spiritual", but in the overall scheme of things it is everyone doing his part that has an impact. You must lay down your rights and become a servant. Determine to do whatever is needed to help further the spread of the gospel among the people you are going to.

Allow the Lord to speak to you

Short-term missions are opportunities for you to experience another culture first-hand and see if God may be calling you there. While on the mission field, set aside time to pray and listen to what God is saying to you. You shouldn't react quickly or superficially to what you see. In order to have God's heart for a city or nation you must pray for it. Prayer is one of the most important and valuable things you can do while on the mission field, and the most important part of prayer is listening. Die to your rights, dreams, and fears. Ask God to call you. Don't resist Him, but plead with Him to break your heart.

If God is saying this is where He wants you, then investigate the opportunities that exist for longer-term service while there. Again, ask God where it is, or what it is He wants you to be doing. Perhaps God will show you the need for some further training to make you more effective before returning to the mission field. There are many things God may reveal to you through the short-term outreach, but the most important thing is that you take the time to listen to what He is saying and don't become so busy that you miss it. After the outreach is over, make sure you return home and report to your leaders or missions committee. Let them debrief you. They helped you go, so you have a special responsibility to go home and serve your church. Be on guard that you don't go back and compare your church with what you experienced on your outreach. Go back to serve, not compare and criticize. If you have trouble adjusting, which happens sometimes, be sure you meet regularly with a mature person in your church to help you work through your adjustments. (More is said about this in Appendix 1 at the end of this book.)

A short-term outreach can be one of the most rewarding experiences you will ever have in life. The key to a successful outreach is preparing yourself ahead of time. The points outlined here will be of great help in doing this and in coming back to your church with a servant's heart.

Is God calling you to take that first step? If so, seek more information and begin to pray with your church leaders now.

Get ready, God is going to change your life!

Chapter Fifteen

Keeping The Fire Burning

Floyd McClung

Has God started a fire burning in your heart?

No fire will burn on continually if left unattended. There will come a time when all the fuel is consumed and the fire ceases to burn. If we want to keep the fire burning we must regularly attend it and stoke it with more fuel.

The same is true of a passion for the Lord, or a missionary calling. If left unattended, it will flicker out or be smothered by other concerns. This chapter is about keeping the call alive and burning in our hearts.

God is concerned about world evangelism and has appointed the church to handle the task. As His church we are all called to the task of reaching the world with the gospel. However, while we're called to evangelize, not everyone is called to be an evangelist. Some are called to plant and establish churches, and others to tend the needs of the poor and destitute. Still others are called to serve as administrators, accountants, computer programmers and operators, personnel directors, graphic artists, mechanics, and cooks. Some are called to go and some are called to be senders. No matter what our profession, God has a place for us in the world of missions.

Hearing the call

"Delight yourself in the Lord; and He will give you the desires of your heart. Commit your way to the Lord, trust also in Him, and He will do it" (Psalm 37:4-5).

We so often complicate guidance and hearing God's voice. Instead of the easy, natural thing it is, we turn it into a maze of complicated detective work in which we often lose our way. But the verses above show how simple the whole process really is.

We are first to delight ourselves in the Lord. To delight in the Lord means to derive pleasure and joy from Him. We want to be with Him. We want to please Him. We want to hear what He has to say to us. And we want to do anything that in turn will bring joy to His heart.

When God sees we delight in Him He will give to us the desires of our hearts. As we have truly delighted ourselves in Him we notice that our desires will change. Our desires begin to have less to do with self, and more to do with what God wants, and how we can please Him. As we look for things that will please Him, one of the things we discover is His consuming passion to see the world evangelized. We read about how He wants all people to come to a knowledge of Him and be saved, and about how He has asked us to cooperate with Him in this task by going into all the world and preaching the gospel. If we have truly delighted ourselves in Him, world evangelism will become one of the desires of our heart.

God will also show us His will for our lives very specifically in the same way. As you put God first, He will give you specific desires in answer to your prayers for direction and guidance. He will cause your desire to grow and He will confirm it in your daily readings of the Bible and through the counsel of godly Christians. Notice, He does not promise you the *objects* of your desires, but the desires themselves!

God wants to release the desires of our heart to us. All He asks is that we commit our way to Him, and trust Him to bring it about. If being involved in world evangelism has become the desire of our heart, then we must commit it to God and trust Him to bring it about. Daily we must do this, and as we do it, we will notice our level of desire grow. As God sees this response from our hearts He will bring it to pass. He will open doors for us and allow us to become involved in reaching the world for Him. We can trust the

Lord to guide us.

Not everyone will be called to full time missionary service, just as not all will be called to be pastors or teachers. Yet there are those who know God has put in their hearts this desire to be involved in world evangelism, and work with Him in completing the great commission.

Where is the mission field?

In a western setting, when we hear the word "mission field", instinctively to our mind come thoughts of tropical jungles and barren deserts where unreached nomadic people wander aimlessly. However, as we have noted in reading this book, the mission field is not somewhere "overseas", it is all about us. All of us as Christians are living on the mission field. There are many "worlds" that make up our world. We have told you about a few of them in this book.

God is shaking up the world. He is bringing the peoples of the world to us for us to minister to. There are vast areas of need within our culture and nation that must also be ministered to. None of us can claim that our nation or culture is fully reached with the gospel. Daily within our neighbourhood people die without knowing Christ. Our neighbour is as much a mission field as someone in India or Kampuchea.

The mission field is all about us. Some of us may be called to go overseas and serve in another nation, others of us may be called to stay at home and serve in our own land. Both are noble callings and we should not consider ourselves some kind of "sub-missionary" if we are called to serve at home. It is not location that makes a missionary, but a heart ready and willing to serve God in doing whatever He asks us to do, and being wherever He asks us to be. So, a person ministering to the poor and needy in New York or London is as much a missionary, and as worthy of support, as the person ministering to the poor and needy in Calcutta or Manila.

This is particularly true because of the Urban World. God is bringing the world to the cities – you can literally reach the whole world in most cities. All of the "worlds" can be found in this one world.

In pursuing the call to missions, we must ask God in what world He wants us to serve. Does He want us in the Hindu world? The Muslim world? The Small Half of the world? The Urban world?

Whoever we are called to serve, whatever "world" we are called to serve in, our calling will be tested. God will grant us the desires of our heart, but we must keep those desires alive and growing.

Keeping the call alive

Only 5% of those who make themselves available for missionary service ever follow through. Why? Because people have allowed the call to die in their hearts. The fire goes out. We must purposely keep the call alive in our hearts if we are to follow through and enter into God's destiny for our lives.

Today's world is very complex and Satan is adept at bringing subtle pressures to bear on our life in the hope that we become side-tracked and unable to follow through with what God has for us. Such pressures come in many ways, such as relationships with people who don't share our sense of call, tying ourselves down financially in an attempt to build future security, getting involved in ministries other than what God has called us to, entering into long-term commitments with business partners, or just plain forgetting about our call through spiritual apathy. They may be small things, and in some cases, justifiable things, but statistics reveal their results – 95% of those called by God to the mission field never make it there.

How do we keep the call alive in our heart?

1) *Keep it alive through single-mindedness.* Start making all your decisions in life in the light of God's calling. This is particularly true when it comes to relationships. If you entertain thoughts of marrying someone who does not share your calling to be a missionary, you are double-minded, and risk the danger of deception. Look for a life partner who has proven his or her dedication to Christ and is enthusiastic about missions.

2) *Keep it burning through prayer.* Get a map of the world and pray over it regularly. Subscribe to mission magazines and prayer letters. Keep prayer lists of missionaries. Read missionary biographies. Put wood on the fire!

Study a particular "world" mentioned in this book. Learn about it and make it a prayer focus. As you do so, your heart will burn with passion. Seek out others with similar interest and pray together.

3) *Consider some form of training to help prepare you.* Such training could range from a six-month discipleship course, to several years of specialized training. What training, if any, you undertake should be decided through prayer and a clear word from the Lord. A good rule to remember as much as possible in this area is that the more practical the training, the better suited it is for the mission field.

God may want you to go to the mission field on a short-term outreach, and while there look at how your interests and skills fit in, and what skills you should learn or develop. When you get home you can set about gaining proficiency in these areas.

In Youth With A Mission we have seen the development of an International University. It has been developed to provide specialized training for those wishing to serve on the mission field. It is based on a modular educational system where a person spends three months learning in the classroom, and then spends another three months in hands-on involvement on the mission field, putting into practice the things learned in the classroom. It is very practical in its approach to learning, and has proved to be very effective.

Education is a two-edged sword and we must be wary of it. While it develops and sharpens new and existing skills, it also has the tendency to puff us up with pride, and cause us to lose sight of why we undertook our training in the first place. Education must not become a god. Education alone will not make us a better or more effective missionary. Education is only a step in getting to where God wants us to be. Be constantly in prayer as you receive further training, and daily remind yourself of the reason for your being in the classroom.

4) *Get out and stay out of debt.* Our "buy-now-pay-later" mentality in the western world has side-tracked many prospective missionaries. We need to learn to say "no" to the pressure our consumer society puts on us to buy. Remain debt-free, and if you currently have debts work as fast as possible toward eliminating them. Most mission societies will not accept people who are burdened down with debt. Learn to become a good steward of all God has given you. And remember, every time you are tempted to buy large or expensive items, evaluate the purchase in the light of the calling God has placed on your heart.

5) *Don't get tied down with attractive offers.* Single-mindedness is the key here. If God has called you to the mission field, rest assured Satan will do all in his power to try and side-track you, and one of the ways he does it is through attractive offers of career, advancement, and investments. Learn to evaluate these offers in the light of world evangelization, and if they interfere with what God is asking of you, reject them.

I heard recently of a young man who felt God was clearly calling him and his family to the mission field. He decided in prayer that on a certain date he would leave his job as a company accountant and pursue his calling. With that conviction in his heart he went off to work. Before he had the opportunity to tell his boss of his decision, the boss came and offered him a new position with the company. It was the job he had dreamed about, the job he had worked toward since he started in accounting. The only requirement for the new job was that he make a minimum of five years commitment to the company. However, this man knew what God had told him to do and declined the attractive offer.

Attractive offers are no substitute for the plan God has for our lives. Again, be single-minded and evaluate all in the light of the calling God has placed on your life.

6) *Get fit.* Good health is essential for the mission field, especially as you learn to adjust to new cultures and climates. Begin to develop good health habits. Eat a balanced diet, and embark upon a regular exercise program.

7) *Go on a short-term mission.* The value of a short-term mission is that you can experience the mission field first-hand, before you make any long-term commitments. You will be able to examine missionaries and mission organizations at work. A short-term mission is often a good place to clarify your calling. Go to the nation or people group to which you feel God is calling you. Observe the people and the missionaries working with them. Pray and ask God to confirm if this is where He wants you and if so, exactly what it is He wants you to be involved in, and with what organization. Through such an experience you will also discover if there are practical things you can learn and do at home to better prepare you before coming back to the mission field long-term. Short-term missions are wonderful opportunities that are guaranteed to give a new spark to the call on your life.

8) *Serve where you are.* The local church is the best place to train for the mission field. There you will learn teachable-ness, diligence, consistency, faithfulness, and wisdom – things you will most assuredly need on the mission field. Take time to talk and counsel with your pastor and church leaders. Tell them about the call God has placed on your

life. Pray with them, and seek their advice as how best to fulfil your calling. Take seriously the counsel they give you, and submit to it. Perhaps they see areas in your life that first need to be dealt with. Perhaps they may require you to become more actively involved in the church program to prove your faithfulness, and your calling. Do it. There is no substitute for the training you will receive in the local church, and if you can't make it in the local church then you will never make it on the mission field. Of course, it is important to do this in a church that is committed to missions and is open in principle to sending you out.

Another benefit we receive from a local church that is committed to promoting and sending missionaries is accountability. For our own protection each of us needs to be accountable to a body of people. The counsel, wisdom, prayer, and pastoral care of the local church offers the accountability we need, both at home and on the mission field.

The tendency in our world today toward doing things "my" way has carried over into the church. This tendency has a name: *independence*. However, independence is not the way of the Kingdom of God. God wants interdependence. Independence destroys unity, interdependence builds it. What we want as we move toward fulfilling our call is to build an interdependent relationship with our local church. We want them to pray for us, care for us, support us, and welcome us back when we come home. In return we want to be accountable to them, and in humility accept any guidance and counsel they may give us. This kind of relationship builds unity and brings great benefit to us and to our local church.

If you are not part of a missionary-minded local church then you need to find one and get involved. You must plant yourself there and build a testimony of faithfulness through manifesting a servant's heart and being loyal. As your desire for missionary service grows, those in the church will see it and will stand with you in prayer and support. This does not happen overnight. It takes time, effort and consistency on your part. J. Hudson Taylor said, "A light that does not shine brightly at home has no business shining anywhere else." If you have a missionary call it is important that you be a part of a church that is committed to missions and open to sending people from the local church to denominational and interdenominational mission programs.

What sort of missionary are you called to be?

For many, the word missionary conjures up the image of a pith-helmeted Englishman hacking his way through the jungle followed by an entourage of natives carrying everything from a grand piano to a teapot. Missionaries today, however, fall basically into four categories, none of which match the above description. It is good to know the category of missionary we feel God is calling us to, as it will allow us to plan and train accordingly.

First, there are *Conventional Missionaries*. These are the missionaries who get involved with long-term cross-cultural missions work. Most often they are involved in evangelism, teaching and discipling, and planting churches in areas where none exist. There are also others in this group working in more defined roles such as Bible translation and medical missions.

Secondly, there are *Support and Logistical Missionaries*. These are the missionaries who are not out in the streets and villages every day evangelizing and discipling Instead they are behind the scenes doing everything from secretarial and clerical work to maintenance, accounting and development work. They are indispensable people who are as much a part of the team as those conventional missionaries out preaching and evangelizing. Without their effort the whole process of evangelism and world missions would grind, very slowly and certainly, to a halt.

Thirdly, there are *Tentmaking Missionaries*. These missionaries enter a country or city, most often closed to missionaries and the gospel, by using a vocation. Often they are involved in such areas as medicine, education, engineering, and business. Through their work and the contacts they make living in the country they are able to share the gospel. This type of missionary is particularly involved in Muslim and communist countries.

Finally, there are *Short-Term Missionaries*. These missionaries can serve anywhere from two weeks to two years. They are the type of people who are mobile and able to go and serve wherever there is a need or manpower shortage. They are people who have come to serve and will do whatever needs to be done. Sometimes they may come for a specific purpose, such as to build a new church or hospital, or to establish a new accounting or computer system.

Is there a place for families on the mission field?

Yes, there is a place for families on the mission field. Indeed, the majority of missionaries serving on the mission field today are married with families. Mission agencies have found that families are not a hindrance to reaching people with the gospel. If anything, they are a help. Children attract other children and have the ability to get into places and relationships that we would not normally be able to get into. They are a wonderful asset when breaking into a new neighbourhood. Children also adjust quickly to the change in culture and location that goes with missionary service. Families tend to bring a sense of stability and maturity to Christian endeavours, particularly in situations where there are large numbers of single missionaries serving.

Perhaps the biggest question facing families who go to the mission field is what to do with their children's education. First, just being on a mission field living in another culture is an educational experience for children. Their horizons will be broadened as they meet and experience – at close quarters – people from another culture. Beyond this, there are a number of different schooling options open to families.

Home Schooling. Depending on the age of the children, some parents may opt to have their children stay at home and be taught by them.

Local Schools. These are usually in the local language and are often the cheapest alternative. An advantage of this type of schooling is that the children get exposure to the language and culture of the country.

International Schools. These schools, held in English, are found in most large cities of the world. While these schools are often expensive, they do maintain continuity with the requirements of the British, and/or American educational systems.

Correspondence School. This is often good for short-term missionaries, especially those from countries where it is illegal for children to be out of school.

Mission Schools. Many Christian organizations and mission agencies run their own schools.

Whatever the solution you choose for your children's education, rest assured there is a place for families on the mission field.

Who Pays?

How missionaries are supported and who pays their expenses vary from mission to mission. As a general rule, though, those who go as short-term missionaries are responsible for the cost of their getting to and from the mission field, as well as their living costs while they are there. Beyond this missionaries may be required to raise their own support, or may be supported by their home church or denomination. Many denominational missions organizations support their missionaries from a unified missions budget, while interdenominational missions agencies ask the missionaries to find a support team who will stand with them for their monthly expenses. Special courses are offered by most agencies to help train their people to do this. Though frightening at first, the advantages of raising your own support are many. For non-westerners, God is giving creative solutions to this challenge.

If God has called you to this mission field, it is important that you begin developing relationships now with a local fellowship or church and with those in that church. Thus, when the time comes for you to fulfil your calling, you will have an established network of relationships with people who will love, support, and pray for you while you are on the mission field.

I pray the steps outlined in this chapter will not only keep the call of God alive in your heart but will also guide you in practical ways as you enter into the destiny God has for your life.

Chapter Sixteen

Mission Agencies – Making The Right Choice

Floyd McClung

The mission agency, as it has become known today, is first noted in its embryonic stage in Acts 13. There we see the development of a simple structure, a missionary team dedicated to the task of preaching the gospel in areas where it has not yet been preached. It is a structure that functions alongside the local church. Although Paul and his team reported back to the church in Antioch, this mission church structure also had a life and leadership of its own that was permanent and respected by the Antioch church. From this simple beginning, through subsequent centuries of church growth and development, this structure has evolved into today's mission agencies.

There have been tensions at times between the local church and the mission agency (see Appendix Two), but I believe the mission agency has survived and developed over time because of its valid function and the benefits it offers the local church.

The mission agency exists to take the gospel cross-culturally to those who have not heard it, and to establish thriving local churches where there previously were none.

Mission agencies offer many benefits to missionaries, such as support and back-up while serving on the mission field, cross-cultural training for adjusting to new cultures and ways of doing things, continuity of work so things don't grind to a halt when someone leaves, and fellowship, community and a sense of identity, while they are separated from their sending church. Local churches simply are not equipped or structured to provide the pastoral support and expertise a mission agency provides thousands of miles from home.

Of mission agencies, Dr Ralph Winter of the U.S. Center for World Missions said "No one has invented a better mechanism for penetrating new social units than the traditional mission society, whether it be Western, African or Asian, whether it be denominational or interdenominational.

Choosing a mission agency to serve with is rather like choosing a new family. Just as we would want to make sure we feel comfortable and belong in the new family before we formally commit ourselves to it, so it is in choosing a mission agency to serve with. The mission agency will, in a sense, become our family and provide the necessary backing, support, and encouragement we need as we serve the Lord, so we will want to be certain of the best possible match, and that the relationship between us and the agency is easy and natural.

Conversely, a mission organization will want to get to know us and make sure we understand and are committed to its objectives and ways of doing things, and, that we are called by God to the mission field and have a desire to serve Him there.

Choosing a mission agency should not be an overwhelming experience. What is important is finding the one where God wants us to be. The process should be pleasant and enjoyable. We want to find a missions agency that we feel comfortable in, that will use our talents and abilities, that is working in the nation or area we feel called to, and that will provide us with the back-up, encouragement and training we need as we serve with it.

Often God will create bridges of friendship to certain agencies. Through friends, family, pastors, and Christian leaders we may become aware of a certain agency's work and develop relationships with people who work with that agency. If this is the case, then this is the place for us to start our search. This is not to say this is the right agency for us, but the process of finding the right agency will be made easier through the friendships we have developed. These friends may also be able to advise us of agencies more suited to our needs and calling.

Outlined below are a number of criteria we should apply as we go through the process of choosing a mission agency to serve with. The list is not intended to be exhaustive and is not intended to replace divine guidance. Each of us will have other personal criteria that we will want to add to the list. The list, however, contains the important issues we should be looking at as we prayerfully select the mission agency God wants us to work with.

1) *What are the mission agency's goals and objectives?* What does the mission agency hope to achieve in the nations where it is working? Does it have a plan and strategy in place to achieve these goals? Are its goals and objectives realistic? Can they be attained, and could you stand behind them and give them your all? Beyond this, will your gifts and talents be put to their best use working toward these particular goals? You must be completely comfortable with, and able to throw yourself behind, an agency's goals and objectives one hundred percent. Otherwise, you will end up in conflict and frustration with the agency.

2) *What countries does the agency serve in?* You will probably be aware of a country or geographic area that you feel God is calling you to. You will want to be certain the agency is working in that nation or area, and that you will be able to serve with them there. However, do not be so rigid about this that you will not listen to any advice a mission agency may offer you in regard to where you should serve. God

may use the agency to further clarify your calling. The country you feel called to may presently be closed to full-time missionaries, but the mission agency may suggest another similar country to serve in, or another nation where there are ethnic groups from the nation you feel called to reach. Be open and flexible, but at the same time don't compromise the calling God has given you by allowing a representative from an agency to talk you into working with them in a place where God clearly hasn't called you to serve.

3) *What activities is the agency involved in?* Are the things the mission is doing the things you feel called to, or which you have the necessary gift to undertake? Again, be open to the advice of the agency, but don't squander any clear leading the Lord has given you. You may be talented at several things but feel God has asked you to concentrate on only one thing. Don't be talked into doing something else you may be good at doing. At the same time be realistic about what it is you feel God wants you to be involved in. Link up with the agency that will allow you to fulfil your calling in the area of activity you feel called to.

4) *Does the agency have a proven track record?* Is the mission successful in what it is doing? Are its goals being achieved? Are those who work for the mission happy and fulfilled in what they are doing? Does the agency have some tangible results it can point to and show you? Each one of us wants to feel our gifts and abilities are being utilized to their fullest, and that we are achieving something as a result of our labor. No one wants to feel he is on a losing team, expending energy, time, and talent with little or nothing to show for it. Look for a missions organization with a proven track record.

Remember, you are looking for a proven track record, not a perfect track record. You will never find a perfect mission agency. All agencies have made, and continue to make, mistakes. What is important is that they have learned from their mistakes and are not continuing to repeat them. What constitutes a proven track record is that the strengths of an agency are enough to compensate for any weaknesses it may have, and there is fruit from their ministry.

Occasionally you will discover an agency that is very young, or is just getting started. It has not had enough time to develop a proven track record. In such cases you should examine the track record of those running or establishing the agency. Do they have a proven track record in relation to the things they have undertaken in the past? If they do, then it is likely the mission agency will, over time, also do well.

5) *How is the mission organized and structured?* Is the mission leadership authoritarian, democratic, or somewhere in between? Is it a one-man, or one-family band? Will your voice be heard and considered when decisions are made? What are its policies in regard to support and finances? Does the mission have an excessive amount of rules, or does it have no rules at all? If you are a woman or from a minority group, what is the agency's attitude toward women and minorities? Could you feel comfortable working under that kind of leadership or organizational structure? Talk to the mission representatives and, if possible, others who work with the mission. Ask them about their relationship with the leadership and organization. Do the staff policies really work? Just because a policy is written in a policy manual does not automatically mean it works in practice. Is there a large gap between what the mission says its policies are and what actually is practised? Remember, ask lots of questions until you are certain about how the mission functions at the grass-roots level.

6) *What is the caliber of the agency's leadership?* How are those who lead the mission agency viewed in the church and community? Are they respected and looked up to? Do they get actively involved in the running of the mission, or do they play a more back-seat role? Ask other Christian leaders and pastors for their assessment of those in leadership of the mission. Ask those who work for the mission

what they think of their leaders. Don't be scared to ask people's opinions; you're not trying to dig up all the dirt you can find on them, but are wanting to know if they are people you could respect, submit to, and work with.

7) *What is the character of those who work with the mission?* One of the greatest recommendations for a mission is the people who work with it. Are they happy and content? Do they feel fulfilled and that their talents and gifts are being put to good use? Do they have confidence in the mission agency and its leadership? Are those who work for the mission well thought-of in the church and community? Are they respected by their peers? Is there a high turnover of staff who leave disgruntled? Find an agency where there is a good morale among the staff and you are well on your way to finding a good mission agency.

8) *What is the financial policy of the mission?* How are those who work for the mission agency supported? How much money do you need monthly to work with the mission? If your support drops off one month, will the mission help carry you or are you totally on your own? Do those who work for the mission find it easy to raise support? Are they generally perceived as worthy of support? You want the financial policy best suited to your needs, and which inspires confidence in the people who support you.

9) *Is the mission flexible?* Once you commit yourself to serve with the mission in a particular area, will the mission allow you to shift to another area or ministry. Often as you grow and develop on the mission field you discover new talents, or see other areas of need that you did not know existed. God may call you to use those new talents or begin ministering to that new area of need. You want to be in an agency that is flexible, that will recognize God is leading you into new areas of ministry, and will free you to pursue it, while at the same time standing behind you with support and encouragement. At a later date, God may call you to serve with another mission agency. Will the agency release you with its blessing to follow the leading of the Lord? It is

important to find an agency that is flexible and willing to release you if they see God is clearly leading you in another direction or to another mission agency.

I talked to a couple recently who joined a particular mission because they sensed the leaders would help develop their gifts as people, even though other agencies seemed to be doing things that matched their areas of interest more. I felt that was a wise approach. Look for a place where you can grow and learn.

10) *What are the history and origins of the mission?* How was the agency started? Was it born out of a particular need, or vision, or did it break away from another organization? If the agency has a published history, read it and any biographies there may be of those who founded the mission. See if the agency has the same zeal as it did when it began. Is the leadership still committed to the founding principles of the mission? Has the mission been effective in the past, is it presently effective, and does it have the potential in staff and leadership to continue to be effective in the future? Above all, ask yourself, could I be excited working for this mission given its past successes, present endeavours, and future potential? Could I give it my all? None of us wants to be involved in an organization that we cannot rake up enthusiasm and excitement for.

11) *Statement of purpose and faith.* What does the mission agency believe? Read its published statement of faith. Do you agree with it? Would you feel comfortable working with an agency that believes these particular things? Are there issues not properly defined where you could come into conflict with the mission agency? Ask questions of the agency and have them try to define more specifically any issues you feel unsure about.

It is vitally important that you be comfortable with, stand fully behind, and wholeheartedly endorse a mission agency's practices and attitudes in relation to doctrine and worship. If you do not feel at peace about them, then be very careful about moving ahead to serve with the agency. If you move ahead while still uncertain about some issues, rest assured at some future time you will run into confrontation with the agency over these issues.

12) *Do you feel a bond developing between you and the agency?* Would you feel comfortable and at home within this mission agency, and would the mission agency feel comfortable having you serve with them? God works through relationship and friendship. It is one of the natural ways He leads us. Where has God given you friendship with people who are "people-oriented"? Look for an organized team that puts people and unity above programs.

It is imperative, however, that you make no commitments to serve with the mission agency until you first have a definite word from God that it is the place where He wants you to be. You must seek Him until He gives you that assurance, or clearly shows you where it is He wants you.

At the same time that you are evaluating the mission agency, the mission agency will also be evaluating you. They want to see if you are the type of missions candidate they are looking for to serve with their organization. Some of the things they will be evaluating you on include:

1) *Your spiritual maturity and preparedness.* The mission agency wants to know you have a mature and growing relationship with the Lord, that you feel called by Him to be involved in missions, and that you have the necessary maturity and wherewithal to follow through on any commitment you may make in fulfilling that calling.

2) *Your qualifications, abilities and talents.* The agency will want to know that you have the necessary qualifications, talents and abilities to be involved in the work they are doing. Or, if you do not, whether you are willing to be trained to meet their requirements. Some agencies will train you themselves, others will ask you to go to seminary or Bible school. Some agencies may require only three to six months of orientation before they send you out to serve with them.

3) *Whether you are teachable and submissive.* Nobody wants

a "know-it-all" working for them, and neither do mission agencies. Often they are working in very sensitive areas of the world and want people who will submit to their leadership and learn from their years of experience what is the best or most effective way to minister in a particular situation. They want people who are submissive and will become part of the team.

4) *A servant's heart.* Regardless of all else, a missionary is first and foremost a servant. We may be well qualified and experienced for a particular task, but we must also be prepared to lay that aside and "wash feet" as a servant if the need should arise. Mission agencies want the people who serve with them to display a servant's heart.

5) *Commitment to the local church.* A missionary is part of a local church. A mission agency helps facilitate the call God has placed upon your life. However, in facilitating that call the agency will want to know you are part of a local church or parish and have proven yourself there through involvement and commitment. If you have not learned the value of commitment in the local church you are unlikely to stay long on the mission field, where commitment and dedication will be tested to the limit. Mission agencies do not want to pour their resources into someone who does not have a proven track record of commitment in the local church.

6) *Your health.* Good physical and mental health are essential to being an effective missionary. Not only is being a missionary a demanding job, but in many instances mission centers are located in areas of the world that are physically demanding as well. So a mission agency will want to know that your health is up to the task.

7) *Your personal integrity.* The various scandals that have rocked some Christian organizations in recent years have forced this issue to the fore. Do you pay your bills on time? Are you known as an honest person in your dealings with others? Do you give your employer an honest day's work? These are the things that the agency wants to know, and they will have employers, church leaders and others fill out

reference forms to attest to your integrity, honesty, and perseverance.

As we started out by saying, choosing a mission agency is like choosing the right family. You want the right family as much as the right family wants you. So you should not be overawed by the points noted in this chapter. Things will flow naturally and God will guide you to the mission agency best suited to you. Mission agencies are as eager to strike the right match as you are and will try their hardest to make the whole process as comfortable and easy as possible. If you take the time to prayerfully search out the agency that is best suited to you, your needs and ministry, you will surely have a long-lasting and fruitful ministry together.

Appendices

Appendix One

The Local Church, The Mission Church And The Great Commission: A Tension Examined

Floyd McClung

There are two streams in church history. The first deals with the preaching of the gospel to every tribe and nation (Matt. 28:18-20), the second deals with the maturing of the saints to be salt and light in a fallen world (Eph. 3 and 4).

At times these two streams have blended together without tension; at other times they have shown little or no sense of accountability and respect towards one another.

Called by different names – the "order" and the "parish", the "mobile church" and the "local church", the "missionary society" and the "denomination", the "apostolic band" and the "local assembly" – the tension is the same, and quite universal.

While the local church or parish is strongly committed to seeing its people become established and take positions of leadership and responsibility, the missionary church is just as committed to challenging those same saints with God's call to go into all the world and preach the gospel to every creature.

The Local Church

This natural tension is heightened, in some circles, by the teaching that the local church is the ideal structure and the only truly biblical expression of the body of Christ. When the local church does its job, the need for the missionary society will be non-existent, so it is said.

In some streams of the charismatic renewal, this teaching has gone so far as to say that in each town there is one anointed church around which all the other churches in that town will eventually gather, somehow becoming an extension of the one "anointed" body.

Others believe in missions, but are strongly convinced that all missionary activity should only be done through the auspices of the local church. They see the biblical pattern as being one of raising up apostolic church-planting teams comprising only well-proven ministries. These teams should be subject to the authority of the local church, no matter how far away they go or how specialized their task.

The Mission Church

At the opposite end of the spectrum, there seems to be a lack of accountability on the part of some missionary societies. The tendency is to feel there is no need to refer to the local church, that if the parishioner wants to join the mission agency, then that is between him and the Lord.

These missionary organizations believe the local church member is accountable only to God for what he does, and though he should inform his pastor or priest of his intentions, he does not need to submit to them fully. The local church tends to be regarded by them as a place to recruit people and raise money. It should train people, send them, support them, and receive them back home when they are tired or needy. There is no real relationship between the mission leader and the pastor of the local church. Because of this, many pastors feel they have virtually no voice in who is recruited from their churches.

The tension examined

Part of the historical tension between the local church and the missionary society has been that on the one hand, the local church does not want all of its resources to be depleted, and on the other hand, the missionary society does not want to lose its autonomy by being totally under the authority of a local church.

The purpose of this appendix is to appeal to church and mission leaders, and to all concerned laymen, to recognize the dangers in allowing this tension to continue without addressing it in a humble and open manner. The church today has never faced greater opportunities for world evangelization, but an unresolved conflict between these two streams of church life will undermine our efforts to respond to the opportunities we have to witness to the world.

We need each other. God has created the church both to nurture local believers and to reach out to a lost world. Local churches and missionary movements that share a spirit of mutual accountability and cooperation will be able to participate in one of the greatest thrusts forward in church history. We are on the threshold of a new surge of church growth, and God is preparing us to be a prophetic voice to the nations. This is the century of the Holy Spirit, and the century is not over yet – the best is yet to come. I believe evangelism is about to rejuvenate the church world-wide in ways we never thought possible.

It is absolutely essential that we act together if we are to see this growth come about. Several important adjustments need to be made in our attitudes and theology in order to allow the church to be the powerful, united force God intends it to be.

(1) We must renounce all attitudes of independence and pride. Any attitude that suggests that our group or church does not need the rest of the body of Christ, or makes us feel we are the precursors of the Kingdom of God in and of ourselves, or that we alone are at the center of what God is doing, is pride. God is at work through many different groups and churches, and many church structures.

Any attitude that does not promote unity, no matter how wrong we feel others are, is sin. When missionary and evangelistic organizations act independently of established and local churches, they only reinforce the worst fears of those church leaders. One perceived wrong is not conquered with another. We must reach out to one another in a spirit of love and trust with a desire to cooperate and serve one another.

(2) We need to develop a much more positive and dynamic ecclesiology. If our view of the church is too small or exclusive, it will result in ignoring or even denying God's blessing on many structures outside our circle of activity and church life. God is working through local church structures and mission church structures. It is His church and He is building it!

I love the church! And God loves the church, too! It is alive, dynamic, growing and powerful. The church is God's work, in all its forms and all its ministries.

The church is the wine and the church structures are the wineskins. Although the wineskins change, the wine does not. While church structures change according to culture, men's gifts, and what God is doing in a particular nation or group, the fact that redeemed people make up the community of God never changes.

God is not a God of methods and formulas, restricted to certain ways of working. While He has used the Anglican church in Singapore (every parish has experienced radical renewal), in the Middle East He used a mission hospital. He is using translation teams as the key to revival in some

Asian nations, and at the same time He is using prayer groups to touch the capital city of a major western nation. What works in one place may not work in another. The Holy Spirit is like a wind that cannot be contained in any man's box, and the church is so dynamic that it cannot be controlled by the theology of any one group.

Missionary movements such as Operation Mobilization, Campus Crusade for Christ, Youth With A Mission, and Wycliffe Bible Translators have experienced great growth and blessing in the past two decades. Between these four groups, 43,000 full and part-time workers were mobilized in 1985 alone, and through their ministries over 2.1 million people indicated they wanted to accept Jesus Christ as their Lord and Savior.

It is important to recognize the blessing on these groups: it is God's way of commending them to the wider church. But they also need to recognize their need of local churches and parishes.

As a leader in a missionary movement, it is my desire for us to be fully supportive of local churches. I want to serve local churches and parishes and help them become the powerful, growing churches their pastors long for them to be. I also want to be accountable to these churches. I believe that as I choose this attitude, and as it is reflected in the actions of our mission, I can help break down any barriers that separate us.

(3)   In order to be the united force God wants us to be, both local churches and missionary organizations need to accept their limitations and the complementary relationship God intends then to have with one another.

Local churches are best at equipping new believers and nourishing them as they serve as salt and light in society. And missionary organizations know how to train people for cross-cultural service. Accepting our limitations and the dependency we have upon one another allows us to inspire and replenish one another.

Each dimension of the church, local and missionary, has a

particular calling. Fulfilling these callings creates a cycle of interdependent activities and mutual blessing. A missionary team goes to an unreached group of people, makes converts, and starts a new fellowship. The new fellowship in turn sends out another team which carries out evangelism resulting in new church life, and so the cycle continues.

In many situations we need missionary teams that do not start new churches but work within established churches to bring renewal. As they equip newly committed Christians for sharing their faith with others, they are fulfilling the great commission as much as if they had started a new church.

(4)   Local churches must not see the great commission as an addendum to the church program. It must be the church program. It is not an optional extra, but the driving force and central vision of the church.

How then does the great commission affect the relationship between the local church and the missionary society? If a local church does not view the great commission as central to all its activities, it will be in a constant struggle with those who do. Those people will feel torn between their commitment to the local church and to missions. But if the local church is consumed with a desire for evangelism, there will be no occasion for divided loyalties among its members.

Missions is a matter of calling, and taking time to test that calling. If a person is called into missionary service, it is only reasonable to expect him to be active in the church's evangelistic activities. Failure to provide those activities is to invite a crisis of loyalty. (This is especially true for young people). However, we should not regard these activities as ways to "keep" more people in church. The church should joyfully embrace the task of training its best to go to other cities and lands and to be sent out of the church to do so. To hold on to people is to lose them in the long run.

Why not develop a positive, well thought-out program which will develop those qualities needed for missionary work rather than force people to feel rebellious for wanting to step out into any form of Christian service outside the local church? A church with this generosity of spirit and broadness of vision will always be flooded with new people, because God can entrust them to its care. The church must view obedience to the great commission as an extension of its own health as a body. Indeed, a church cannot consider itself truly renewed or restored if it does not have this view of the great commission.

(5) Local churches and missionary organizations should develop well thought-out policies of how they will relate to each other and what they expect of one another. Establishing mission committees and/or appointing a particular person to be responsible for missions in the local church will help channel those who want to serve. The church that does not make missions its future has no real future. The future of both the church and the world is wrapped up in loving the whole world with God's love. To love the world in this sacrificial way is absolutely essential if we are going to be instruments in God's hands to see it changed.

For more information on how to establish a missions committee and to form missions policies in the local church, please write to the Evangelical Missionary Alliance in your nation, or contact:

ACMC
P.O. BOX ACMC
Wheaton, IL 60189-8000
USA

Appendix Two

Short-Term Missions
And The Local Church

Floyd McClung

Although God is using short-term mission experiences to deepen the commitment to world evangelization in the hearts of young and old alike, there are difficulties that can arise if the local church and the mission organization channelling people into short-term service do not cooperate to see God's maximum blessing for the church, the mission and the individual.

While serving in another culture, the short-term volunteers can see first-hand some of the lostness of the world as well as some of the hurts and the needs that exist in other cultures. As a result, they will return home with a new sense of dedication to God and a new fire burning in their hearts to make their lives count for God.

Some of these short-term workers feel called to go on to a career of missionary service. Others find it obvious that what they thought was a missionary call was human enthusiasm. Still others become significantly involved in the on-going mission thrust of the church, where God can use their experience as a spark to light others with a commitment to world evangelization.

Unfortunately, still other short-term workers do not remain actively committed to mission for the local church. Why? Their enthusiasm for world mission is dulled by the pressures they face when they return home. They do not integrate the blessings of the short-term experience into practical service in the local church. *How can the local church and the missionary organization encourage these individuals to stay vitally involved in world evangelization? And how can they be encouraged and challenged for effective service in the local church when they return?*

The following suggestions are made to help initiate positive policies in the local church to guide those who want to be involved in short-term mission experiences. These policies *should not* be used to control people or keep them back from service, but to give them guidelines and let them understand what the local church expects from them if they are going to be sent out with the blessing of the church. In this way people can understand clearly what is required of them and will be a practical help in preparing them for their return after the short-term experience.

Obviously the burden is not entirely on the local church to make the short-term experience meaningful. It is a matter of mutual accountability between the local church and the mission agency to see God's full blessing realized in the lives of all those involved. It is with this in mind that we make the following suggestions to help make the short-term experience for the person going out from the church all that God wants it to be.

These suggestions are made in three different stages:

1. Screening and Stewardship

A. Each local church should develop its own mission policies. This would include developing a manual or paper that outlines the policies and who is responsible (such as Pastor of Missions or Missions Committee) to implement the policies. In other words, if someone wants to go out in short-term service, the pastor can refer him to the Missions Committee or the Pastor of Missions. The policies should give the qualifications the short-termer must meet, the church's philosophy of missions and the process for application for those to be sent out with the church's blessing. In this way, the burden is taken off the pastor or the leadership of the church to make decisions on an individual basis as to whether or not people can be involved. For example, if someone wants to be involved in a short-term missions project, but has not been faithful in attendance in the local church, has never offered to help in teaching Sunday School, or has not been available to do practical responsibilities when asked, it can be pointed out that the policy of the church states that the church will back only those who are active and consistent in attendance and service. The standards should not be too strict or people will never be able to attain them, but they should involve some sacrifice. This gives the church a chance to screen those who are going out.

Perhaps the reason some people don't integrate successfully back into the local church is *because they were not mature when they went out.* If the local church takes more responsibility for screening those who do go out, then it is more likely that when people come back from a short-term experience they will feel more accountability to the local church.

B.   Every person involved in short-term missions should be encouraged to view themselves as *stewards* of their short-term experience. These experiences are not only for personal edification, career guidance, or a one-time contribution to mission, but are also given to individuals by God to be used for the good of the local church. Short-term workers need to build what they have learned into the lives of others and help the local church move forward in missions. This means the short-term workers should be given orientation and instruction before they are selected and sent out by the local church. Those not presently involved in the life of the church, or not willing to be multipliers of the vision upon their return, are not the best candidates for the church's investment. Short-term workers should view themselves as stewards of their experiences for the good of the entire Body.

C. The church's involvement financially for those going out in short-term experiences will obviously vary from church to church, depending on the size of the church, the maturity of the person, how long he has been actively involved in the church, and how many short-termers may be going out at any one time.

A basic rule-of-thumb that many churches have found to work well is to ask those who are going to summer programs, Bible School, or other training programs, to be responsible to raise their own finances. (Obviously the church may wish to encourage its members to give to those going out in these situations, but still recognize the responsibility of those going to pay their own way.) The church can make it clear that its commitment is to help raise support for those doing long-term missions, or one or two year short-term commitments. In this way the church is making financial investments in those who have shown initiative and responsibility, and have proven themselves in the church and in short-term endeavors.

2. Orientation and preparation

A. It's helpful for the local church to give orientation to those who are going out in short-term experience as to what the church's view of missions is, what the church expects of the people while they are involved (i.e. reports, letters, etc.) and the adjustments the short-termers should expect as they go into a new situation or culture. It's very helpful for the local church to have those who have had missionary experience give training to people as to what they will experience when they leave home and go to another nation. Materials may be available from the mission agency to help with the task.

B.   One pastor I know reminds young people that when they go out, their accountability is to the authority of the local church and that he does not want them making any long-term decisions until they report back to the local church. They will review, upon their return (through the Missions Pastor or Missions Committee), how beneficial their experience was, how well they did when they were in the mission experience and how well they integrate back into the local church. This kind of oversight, preparation and orientation produces not only a better prepared candidate, but also a greater level of accountability in people's lives to the Lord and the local church.

3. The re-entry process

A. It is the responsibility of both the mission agency and the local church to prepare its volunteers for the re-entry process into the local church. Short-term workers need to be adequately debriefed and helped to process their experiences upon their return. It is the responsibility of the mission to remind the short-term workers that they should not compare their experience on the short-term situation (where they have experienced many hours of prayer, evangelism, relationship building, worship, etc.) with the life of the local church. There are two different structures involved: the missions structure and the local church structure. God raised up both for different purposes. It's too easy for people to compare the mission experience with the life of the local church and draw negative conclusions. People are to be reminded of God's purpose for the local church. It provides the nurture and resources for 95 percent of all of God's people! This means that all of those involved in 9 a.m. to 5 p.m. jobs, who are salt and light in the world, are called by God to be there. It is important to remind the short-termer (and to actively teach and practise) that the local church is also a mission structure, called to support those who have been led by God to serve Him as His ambassadors in the work world. Sometimes it is much easier to be involved in foreign missions than it is to be involved in the business world, in the factory, or in the local shop. They need to be reminded of the vital place that the local church plays in world missions and helped to develop a positive ecclesiology.

B.   When the short-term workers return to the local church, they need to be able to discuss what they saw God do, things that changed their attitudes, perspectives and priorities, and what they learned about their gifts and abilities. These subjects need to be dealt with lovingly, carefully and with others who can help the short-term workers evaluate and respond to their findings.

Short-term workers need people from their local church who will listen reflectively over a period of months as they integrate their new experiences into their home culture. *We suggest that somebody be appointed from the local church to meet with those who have been involved in short-term missions on a weekly basis for prayer, counselling, and for reflection so that they can successfully integrate back into the life of the church.* They need those who will understand what they are feeling and encourage them in the learning process. They need individuals who will direct them toward practical ways to become catalysts for missions in the church. Meeting and sharing with others who represent the leadership of the church and *who have a positive view toward the church and missions* can be extremely useful in helping people reintegrate back into the local church. There will be adjustments. It is natural to come back excited and anxious to share with others. Encourage this enthusiasm, but also be there to help when the zeal dies down and they return to school or work. This let-down can be accompanied by criticalness and comparisons, but if challenged and guided as they work through these adjustments, tremendous growth can take place. We recommend that local churches send elders or mature members on short-term outreaches so they understand first-hand the experiences of their members.

C. It is also important for the local church to have programs that challenge the young people and other short-term workers for constructive service once they come back to the local church. When the short-term workers come back fired up and there is no opportunity for service, they can become disillusioned and disappointed. One local church started an evangelism program that went into effect in September for all those who came out of short-term summer experiences. This puts the responsibility back on the short-term worker not to be critical of the local church, but to "put their money where their mouth is!" It also puts responsibility on the church to lead by example.

D. Short-term workers also need positive, objective feedback in writing about their experiences (a simple evaluation form) shown to them before their outreach and completed after their return. This can be useful in helping them to evaluate their growth and how the church sees them. This will show the short-term workers how others see their strengths and weaknesses and help direct them toward areas to work on in preparation for future ministry. If the local church also requests an evaluation from the mission on how the worker did, it can be helpful in this feedback process. This long-range re-entry process is the responsibility of both the local church and the mission agency. The mission organization obviously has a great responsibility in this process, *but because people come out of the local church, the church must take primary responsibility for the re-entry process.*

Conclusion

When church workers are screened properly, orientated by the local church, taught that they are stewards of short-term experiences, and have a re-entry process that has been established, the fires that have been lit in the lives of short-term missionaries can continue to burn. Some practical steps can be taken to keep those fires burning in the hearts of those who feel called:

1. They should share with the leadership of the local church the burden on their heart and they should be encouraged to develop it. Opportunity should be given to do this on a regular basis so the church is not surprised when it learns of this desire in a letter sent from Mexico or Europe! Aspiring missionaries and enthusiastic short-termers should be told the church wants to encourage them but does not want surprises! As the church takes initiative with its members, it has maximum opportunity to counsel them and influence them in their decisions and preparations.

2. They should read missionary biographies that will help inspire them to believe that God can use them.

3. They should be encouraged to faithful service in the local church.

4. The local church should challenge them to be involved in mission outreaches in the local area, in nearby cities, states, and in other countries to keep them actively involved in witnessing and sharing their faith.

5. They should be encouraged to stay out of debt.

6. They should be counselled to marry someone who has a similar calling on his or her life.

7.   They should get on the mailing list of several mission agencies to keep prayer information in front of them

8.   They should be encouraged to intercede regularly for the lost and for the nations of the world. It would be helpful to read P.J. Johnstone's book, "Operation World", and to use Youth With A Mission's "Prayer Diary" (which serves as a practical diary for appointments and addresses, and also lists all the nations of the world for prayers as well as helpful information about quiet times, Bible meditation, and intercession).

9.   They should write to various mission agencies to familiarize themselves with the different programs, philosophies and approaches to missions so that they can pray intelligently about which one they should be involved in. (See Appendix Three for mission agencies and addresses that you can write to for more information.)

Appendix Three

Mission Agency Address List

AFRICA INLAND MISSION (AIM)
USA: P.O. Box 178, Pearl River, New York 10965.
UK: 2 Vorley Road, Archway, London N19 5HE.
AUST: 36 Hercules Street, Chatswood, NSW 2067.
NZ: 144 White Swan Road, Auckland 4.

ASIAN OUTREACH
HONG KONG: GPO Box 3448.
USA: PO Box 9000, Mission Viejo, California 92690.
UK: 2 Kingswood Close, Lytham, Lancs FY8 4RE.
NZ: PO Box 2160, Tauranga.

ASSEMBLIES OF GOD
USA: Division of Foreign Missions, 1445 Boonville Avenue,
Springfield, Missouri 65802.
UK: 106/114 Talbot Street, Nottingham NG1 5GH.
AUST: PO Box 229, Nunawading, Victoria 3131.
NZ: PO Box 8023, Tauranga.

BETHANY FELLOWSHIP MISSIONS
USA: 6820 Auto Club Road, Minneapolis, Minnesota 55438.

CAMPUS CRUSADE FOR CHRIST
USA: Arrowhead Springs, San Bernardino, California 92414.
UK: 103 Friar Street, Reading, Berks RG1 1EP.
NZ: 73 Khyber Pass Road, Auckland 3.

CHRISTIAN LITERATURE CRUSADE (CLC)
USA: PO Box C, Fort Washington, Pennsylvania 19034.
UK: 201 Church Road, London SE19 2PT.
AUST: PO Box 91, Pennant Hills, New South Wales 2120.

CHRISTIAN & MISSIONARY ALLIANCE (CMA)
USA: PO Box C, Nyack, New York 10960.
CAN: PO Box 7900, Station B, Willowdale,
Ontario M2K 2R6.
AUST: 86 The Esplanade, French's Forest,
New South Wales 2086.

FAR EAST BROADCASTING COMPANY (FEBC)
USA: PO Box 1, La Mirada, California 90637.
AUST: PO Box 183, Caringbah, New South Wales 2229.
NZ: PO Box 4140, Hamilton.

MISSION AVIATION FELLOWSHIP (MAF)
USA: PO Box 202, Redlands, California 92373.
UK: Ingles Manor, Castle Hill Avenue, Folkestone,
Kent CT20 2TN.
AUST: PO Box 211, Box Hill, Victoria 3128.
NZ: PO Box 611, Manurewa, Auckland.

THE NAVIGATORS
USA: PO Box 6000, Colorado Springs, Colorado 80934.
UK: Tregaron House, 27 High Street, New Malden,
Surrey KT3 4BY.
AUST: PO Box A-143, Sydney South,
New South Wales 2000.
NZ: PO Box 1951, Christchurch.

NEW TRIBES MISSION
USA: 1000 E. First Street, Sanford, Florida 32771.
UK: Derby Road, Matlock Bath, Matlock,
Derbyshire DE4 3PY.
AUST: PO Box 84, Rooty Hill, New South Wales 2766.
NZ: PO Box 2339, Christchurch.

OPEN DOORS
NETHERLANDS: PO Box 47, 3840 AA Harderwijk.
USA: PO Box 2006, Orange, California 92669.
UK: PO Box 6, Standlake, Witney, Oxon OX8 7SP.

OPERATION MOBILIZATION (OM)
USA: PO Box 148, Midland Park, New Jersey 07432.
UK: The Quinta, Western Rhyn, Oswetry,
Shropshire SY10 7LT.
AUST: 62 Glengale Drive, Rochedale, Brisbane,
Queensland 4123.

OVERSEAS MISSIONARY FELLOWSHIP (OMF)
USA: 404 South Church Street, Robesonia,
Pennsylvania 19551.
UK: Belmont, The Vine, Sevenoaks, Kent TN13 3TZ.
AUST: 14 Grange Road, Kew, Victoria 3103.
NZ: PO Box 10-159, Auckland 4.

OMS INTERNATIONAL
USA: PO Box A, Greenwood, Indiana 46142.
UK: 1 Sandleigh Avenue, Didsbury, Manchester M20 9LN.
NZ: PO Box 962, Hamilton.

SOUTH AMERICAN MISSIONARY SOCIETY (SAMS)
UK: Allen Gardiner House, Pembury Road,
Tunbridge Wells TN2 3QU.
AUST: 25 Alexander Parade, Roseville,
New South Wales 2069.

SIM INTERNATIONAL
USA: PO Box C, Cedar Grove, New Jersey 07009.
UK: Joint Mission Centre, Ullswater Cres., Coulsdon,
Surrey CR3 2HR.
AUST: PO Box 171, Summer Hill, New South Wales 2130.
NZ: PO Box 38-588, Howick, Auckland.

SOUTH SEA EVANGELICAL MISSION
AUST: 12a Coronation Street, Hornsby,
New South Wales 2077.
NZ: PO Box 67010 Mt. Eden 3, Auckland.

THE EVANGELICAL ALLIANCE MISSION (TEAM)
USA: PO Box 969, Wheaton, Illinois 60189.
CAN: PO Box 980, Regina, Saskatchewan S4P 3B2.
AUST: 26 Homebush Road, New South Wales 2140.

WYCLIFFE BIBLE TRANSLATORS
USA: Huntington Beach, California 92647.
UK: Horsldeys Green, High Wycombe, Bucks HP14 3XL.
AUST: Graham Road, Kangaroo Ground, Victoria 3097.
NZ: PO Box 10, Featherston, Wairarapa.

WORLD EVANGELISTIC CRUSADE INTERNATIONAL
(WEC)
USA: PO Box 1707, Fort Washington, Pennsylvania 19034.
UK: Bulstrode, Gerrards Cross, Bucks SL9 8SZ.
AUST: 48 Woodside Avenue, Strathfield,
New South Wales 2135.
NZ: PO Box 27264, Mt. Roskill, Auckland 4.

WORLD RADIO MISSIONARY FELLOWSHIP
(Radio HCJB)
USA: PO Box 3000, Opa Locka, Florida 33055.
UK: 7 West Bank, Dorking, Surrey RH4 3BZ.
NZ: PO Box 27-172, Auckland 4.

WORLD VISION INTERNATIONAL
USA: 919 W. Huntington Drive, Monrovia,
California 91016.
AUST: PO Box 399 C, Melbourne, Victoria 3001.
NZ: PO Box 1923, Auckland 1.

YOUTH WITH A MISSION (YWAM)
USA: President's Office, 75-5851 Kuakini Highway,
Kailua-Kona, Hawaii 96740.
Office of the Americas, PO Box 4600, Tyler, Texas 75712.
UK: Europe, Middle East, and Africa Office,
13 Highfield Oval, Ambrose Lane, Harpenden,
Herts. AL5 4BX.
JAPAN: Pacific and Asia Office, 1405 Monoi,
Yotsukaido-shi, Chiba 284.
NETHERLANDS: International Operations Office,
Samaritan's Inn, Prins Hendrikkade 50,
1012 AC Amsterdam.
MERCY SHIPS: PO Box YWAM, San Pedro,
CA 90733, USA.

LIVING ON THE DEVIL'S DOORSTEP
Floyd McClung

Just an ordinary young couple from American suburbia - but they dared to dream they could make a difference.

Their dream took them all over the world: first to the backstreets of Kabul, Afghanistan and later to the bright lights of Amsterdam's Red Light District.

Share in their adventures, their heartaches and their joys as they reach out to people in need - sharing their home with hippies in Kabul or working amongst addicts, prostitutes and Aids victims in Amsterdam.

With their two children, Floyd and Sally McClung still live 'on the Devil's Doorstep' where God is at work bringing hope to hopeless people.

Their story will speak to all those who want help and inspiration for their lives.

Catalogue Number YB 9142   £2.95

WHY SETTLE FOR MORE AND MISS THE BEST?
Tom Sine
author of The Mustard Seed Conspiracy

'The call to recognize that the foolishness of the Gospel is more reasonable in the end than the wisdom of this world... A better way to find joy and meaning in life.'
From the Foreword by TONY CAMPOLO

LINKING YOUR LIFE TO THE PURPOSE OF GOD
Is your life a frenetic dash from one thing to another? Have you forgotten what it's all for?

'God created us and God calls us to meaning,' asserts Tom Sine. 'We are called to climb a better mountain.' Probing behind the contemporary lifestyles, he shows how our lives are often limited by our own assumptions and the expectations of others. Instead, he challenges us to discover and follow God's dream for us, so that we can live lives of celebration, discovery and purpose.

'A vital message for every lay person and Christian leader in the Western world. Please don't pass by this book.' *Floyd McClung, Founding Director, Youth with a Mission*

'Exciting and insightful, penetrating and prophetic.'
Dr Myron Augsburger, author and speaker

'Has helped me rethink, revise, and rekindle my passion to live Christianity in the 1980's.'
Rebecca Manley Pippert, author and speaker

TOM SINE is a staff member and consultant at World Concern. A prolific writer, he also works with churches in the area of futures research and planning. He has a doctorate in American intellectual History from the University of Washington and is a popular lecturer.

Catalogue No. YB9302 £2.95